The Let's Series of ESL

LET'S READ

Phase Two

William Samelson

ELSTREET
EDUCATIONAL
Baltimore • Washington

ELSTREET
EDUCATIONAL

An imprint of Bartleby Press
PO Box 858
Savage, MD 20763
(800) 953-9929
www.Elstreet.com

Cover Illustrations by Edward Molina
Cover Design by Ross Feldner

Library of Congress Cataloguing-in-Publication Data

Samelson, William, 1928-
  Let's read. Phase two / William Samelson.
    pages cm. -- (The Let's Series of ESL; Phase 2)
  Includes bibliographical references and index.
  ISBN 978-0-935437-32-4 (alk. paper)
  1. English language--Textbooks for foreign speakers. 2. English language--Rhetoric--Problems, exercises, etc. I. Title.
  PE1128.S21764 2013
  428.2'4--dc23

                                                    2013029136

Printed in the United States of America

To David Lozano, dear friend and benefactor

Contents

Preface

This is a significantly updated version of the previous edition of Let's Read. Although the changes of this second edition are not extensive, they are extremely important, because they provide the student with additional tools for learning to read and comprehend everyday American English which were not present in the original text. These modifications came about as a result of many years of classroom experimentation as well as suggestions from colleagues in the continental United States and those abroad who have successfully used the original text of Let's Read.

The revision and changes in the original text cut across some crucial aspects of learning aids, including vocabulary revision and amplification, structural exercises, graphic presentations, and many others. Of special interest is the addition of marginally annotated vocabulary for each Narrative section. To aid the student in self-expression a set of IDEA QUESTIONS was added following the Narrative. This will help students to crystallize thoughts about the material read and elicit personal responses from each student. Also an added feature is the expanded Table of Contents which pinpoints each aspect of study. The addition of a table of Principal Parts of Irregular Verbs and Parts of Speech as well as an amplified vocabulary section complete the most significant revisions.

Of course, my expression of gratitude to all those who have helped me with the first edition remains unchanged. However, I would like to extend special thanks to my colleagues, friends and students who have offered some constructive criticism and helped to include those items which make the present edition a more useful tool for the study of reading comprehension.

Acknowledgements

Needless to say, I owe a debt of gratitude to many for their generous contributions to the preparation of this text: to such scholars as Jespersen, Politzer, Fries, Croft, and Dykstra who have influenced my thinking through their works.

Introduction

A listing of some common grammatical terms is in order.

I. Parts of Speech

We recognize in every sentence, words that fulfill a specific function. Such words are called *parts of speech*. There are basically **eight** such words : (1)noun, (2), verb, (3) pronoun, (4) adjective, (5) adverb, (6) preposition, (7)conjunction, and (8) interjection.

A. **Noun**-means a person (*Abraham Lincoln*); place (*Illinois*); thing [animal or object] (*lion, book*); quality (*wisdom*); state (*honesty, sadness*); or action (*exercise, play*). A common marker of a noun is the determiner "the" or "a."

B. **Verb**-expresses action (*study, run*); state of being or condition (*be, is*).

C. **Pronoun**-takes the place of a noun phrase *(he, she, it, we, you, they)*.

D. **Adjective**-modifies, describes, or limits the noun (*good* man, *bad* student; *many* things).

E. **Adverb**-modifies the verb (read slowly), adjective (*extremely* slow), or adverb (*very* quickly).

F. **Preposition**-shows the relationship between a noun or pronoun and another word (water *under* the bridge, think *before* speaking).

G. **Conjunction**- joins words or groups of words (Rose *and* Bill, it's good to be poor in money *but* rich in spirit.)

H. **Interjection**-shows emotion (*Gosh!*, *Damn!*), an exclamation of surprise (*Oh! Gee!*), delight (*Wow! Hurrah!*), etc.

II. The Sentence

The sentence consists of a group of words that present a meaningful thought. It is classified according to its use or function. The sentence contains two main parts : noun phrase + verb phrase. There are five major types of sentences.

A. **Declarative Sentence (Statement)**
   He studies English. (Affirmative)
   He doesn't study English. (Negative)

B. **Interrogative (Word Question) Sentence**
   Why does he study English?
   Where does he study English?

C. **Imperative (Command, Request) Sentence**
   Give me the book!
   Study English!

D. **Exclamatory Sentence (Expresses Emotion)**
   What a nice day!

III. The Paragraph

There is no set rule for the number of words or sentences a paragraph must contain. The most common paragraph, however, links several related sentences. These sentences should focus on the same topic; they clarify, amplify, and defend it.

The following is a typical paragraph :

A topic sentence usually comes first in the paragraph. It contains the main idea of the paragraph. The rest of the paragraph consists of sentences which support the topic sentence. Some sentences refer directly to the topic sentence. Others may expand the ideas of the topic sentence.

A road warning sign may serve as an illustration of a paragraph:

> ATTENTION!
> THIS ROAD IS UNDER CONSTRUCTION.
> PROCEED WITH CAUTION. MEN AT
> WORK. SPEED LIMIT 20 MPH. THE LIFE
> YOU SAVE MAY BE YOUR OWN!

An advertising poster may serve as an example of a short visual paragraph (**pictograph**):

IV. Key to Word Recognition

A. Some Common Prefixes and Roots

By knowing the meaning of prefixes, roots, and suffixes, and being able to combine them, one may often be able to determine the meaning of a word. The following are only a few examples of such word components. They are listed here in the hope that this knowledge will enable the student to learn a whole word family when learning a new word. For example, from the word *dramatize* we can learn *dramatization, dramatist, dramaturgy,* etc.

PREFIX	GENERAL MEANING	ROOT	GENERAL MEANING	EXAMPLE
circum-	around	*nav*	sail, ship	circumnavigate
de-	away from, down	*tain*	hold	detain
dis-	opposing, apart from, not, off	*pos*	put, place	dispose
epi-	on, over, upon, near, beside	*gram, graph*	writing	epigram, epigraph
intro-	between, among	*duc*	lead	introduce
mal-	bad	*vol*	wish	malevolent
mis-	wrong	*anthrop*	man, mankind	misanthrope
over-	excessive, above	*dra*	do, act	overdramatize
pre-	before	*clude*	close, shut	preclude
sub-	under, below, beneath	*vers, vert*	turn	subvert
syn-	with, together	*onym*	name	synonym
trans-	beyond, over, across	*fus*	pour	transfusion
uni-, mono-	one, alone	*form, gamy*	shape, marriage	uniform, monogamy

CHAPTER ONE

Friends Meet

IN THIS CHAPTER

Words to Remember:
Present time—Habitual action
General action—Present condition

Personal Pronouns:
I, you, he, she, it, we, you, they

Declarative Sentence and Determiners:
a, an, the

Possessives:
my, your, our, his, their

Demonstratives:
this, that, these, those

I. Narrative

A. It is an early morning class. The students assemble in the class-room. They wait for their teacher, Mr. Preston. He is late for class. He is delayed on his way to school because there is a traffic jam on the freeway.

B. Mr. Preston arrives five minutes later. The students are eager to begin their lesson. They study English. The students need to learn the language of the land. They come from many parts of the world, and they don't know each other by name. Mr. Preston tells the students to stand up as they tell their names.

C. There are Gloria Nave and Arturo Silva. They are new Americans. There is also Marcel Boileau. Marcel comes from Paris, France. Gloria thinks Marcel has a funny name. The students laugh. They are unable to pronounce his name the way he does. Marcel is glad to be in the United States.

D. Marcel has many relatives in France. He visits them during vacation. He likes his American friends. Some of his classmates plan their vacations early. They all like to travel.

E. Mr. Preston shows some places on the map of America. Marcel points out places to visit on the map of France. The lesson is interesting, and all students get acquainted.

F. After the lesson, the students go to the cafeteria. They meet there often after classes. It has a relaxed atmosphere. They talk while they eat. Some students don't talk. They just listen. You can learn about many things when you listen well. They talk about customs. People have different customs, but they are friendly. Marcel likes his friends.

---

early: near the beginning
wait: stay (in place)
late: not on time
traffic: overcrowding
arrive: come
visit: to go to see (someone)

during: at the time (of)
plan: arrange
cafeteria: self-serve restaurant
customs: traditons
different: not the same, distinct.

Idea Questions:

1. Where do the students wait?
2. Where is Mr. Preston delayed?
3. Why is Mr. Preston late?
4. Why are the students eager to learn English?
5. Where do the students come from?
6. Why do the students stand up?
7. Why does Marcel go to France?
8. Where do the students go after class?
9. Why do the students like the cafeteria?
10. What is the MAIN IDEA in paragraph "F"?

II. Words in Context (Pictographs)

Below are some of the words used in the narrative. Where possible, each word has a [synonym] , or it is defined as used in the story. Where possible, an *(antonym)* is also given. Make up sentences about the pictographs choosing the words you need. Read aloud.
Example : [group of students] = There is a group of students.

A. B. and C.

morning [**early in the day**] *(evening)*; class [**group of students**]; assemble [**gather**]; teacher [**instructor**]; delay [**detain**]; freeway [**expressway**]; classroom [**schoolroom**]; eager [**anxious**]; need [**want**]; begin [**start**] *(finish)*; part [**section**]; stand up [**get up**]; know [**be acquainted with**]; come [**arrive**] *(leave)*; think [**reason**]; funny [**strange**] *(serious)*; laugh [**chuckle**] *(cry)*; to be unable [**cannot**]; pronounce [**articulate**]; glad [**happy**] *(sad)*

D. E. and F.

many [**a lot of**] *(few)*; relative [**family**]; vacation [**rest**] *(work)*; like [**fond of**] *(dislike)*; friend [**ally**] *(enemy)*; classmate [**fellow student**]; travel [**journey**];place [**locality**]; show [**point out**]; interesting [**fascinating**]; get acquainted with [**meet**]; often [**frequently**] *(seldom)*; relaxed [**comfortable**]; atmosphere [**feeling**]; listen [**hear**]; friendly [**amicable**]

Drawing of Paragraph A, B & C in Dialogue

III. Structures [Phrases]

Below are some phrases taken from the narrative. Make sentences and read them aloud.

1. assemble—in—the classroom
2. for—their—teacher
3. late—for—class
4. on—his—way
5. need—to—learn
6. of—the—land
7. of—the—world
8. to—stand up
9. they—tell—names
10. to—pronounce
11. glad—to—be
12. places—to—visit
13. after—the—lesson
14. while—they—eat
15. because—you—listen

Drawing of Paragraph D, E & F in Dialogue

IV. Sentences

A. Read the following sentence aloud. Repeat, substituting where possible, the synonym of the word in italics, or a phrase that explains the meaning. Make other necessary changes.

> Example: It is a *class.*
>   It is a *group of students*

1. The students *assemble.*
2. He is *delayed.*
3. Mr. Preston is on the *freeway.*
4. Mr. Preston *arrives.*
5. The students are *eager.*

6. They don't *know* each other.
7. Marcel has a *funny* name.
8. Marcel is *glad* to be in the United States.
9. He likes his *friends*.
10. Mr. Preston shows some *places*.
11. The lesson is *interesting*.

B. Fill in the following blanks with words from the narrative. Each space may be filled by a word or phrase. Do not refer back to the narrative. Where possible, use variations of the missing words. Read aloud.

It is an _____ morning_____. The students _____ in the _____.
They _____ for their _____. Mr. Preston is _____ for _____. He is _____ on his _____ to school _____ there is a _____ on the _____.

Mr. Preston _____ five _____ later. The _____ are _____ to _____ their lesson. They _____ English. They _____ from _____ parts of the _____. The students don't _____ each other. The students _____ while they _____ their names.

Gloria and Arturo are _____. Marcel _____ from France. Marcel has a _____ name. The students are _____ to pronounce his name and they _____.

Marcel has _____ in France. He _____ them during _____. Some of his _____ plan to _____ France. The students _____ to _____ Mr. Preston _____ the _____ of America. Marcel _____ out _____ to visit in France. The lesson is _____ and all _____ get _____.

After the _____, the students _____ to the _____. They _____ there often _____ classes. It is a _____ atmosphere. Some students _____ _____. Students talk _____ customs. People _____ different _____.

V. Grammar (Points of Interest)

A. **The Simple Present Tense** expresses PRESENT TIME, GENERAL ACTION, HABITUAL ACTION, and PRESENT CONDITION.

The students *wait* for Mr. Preston. (PRESENT TIME)
He *is* late for class. (PRESENT TIME)
They *study* English. (GENERAL ACTION)
They *wait* for Mr. Preston each morning. (HABITUAL ACTION)
They *are* unable to pronounce his name. (PRESENT CONDITION)
Marcel *is* glad to be in the United States. (PRESENT CONDITION)

B. The **Personal Pronoun** refers to the
1. SPEAKER (the person(s) who speak(s)—*I or we*).
2. the PERSONS Spoken to—*you.*
    You can learn about many things.
3. the PERSON or THING being SPOKEN of (*he, she, it, they*).
    He comes from France   *It* is early.
    She studies English.   *They* all like to travel.

C. A **Declarative Sentence** makes, or denies, a statement. It has as its normal word order: the SUBJECT [Noun Phrase] and the PREDICATE [Verb Phrase]. The sentence ends with a period.

D. Twelve words have the function of **Noun Determiners**.
They are: ARTICLES: *a, an, the*
                 POSSESSIVES: *my, your, our, his, their*
                 DEMONSTRATIVES: *this, that, these, those*

He's a student.
This is an early morning class.
The teacher is delayed.
My relatives live in France.
They plan *their* vacation early.

Note: the **Non**definite article *a* is commonly used before words beginning with a consonant sound: *a* student, *a* relative, etc. *An* is used before words that being with a vowel sound: *an* American, *an* early class, etc. There are some exceptions: *an* honor, *a* university, etc.

E. The **Compound Sentence** has two or more full PREDICATIONS in the form of independent clauses. The clauses are frequently connected by words (CONJUNCTIONS) such as *and, but, for, nor, or, so, yet.*

It is an early morning class *and* the students assemble.
The teacher is late *for* there is a traffic jam.
The students stand up *as* they tell their names.

VI. Word Recognition

A. Circle the word or phrase in Column II that is most *like* the word in Column I, and the word or phrase in column III that is most *unlike* the word in Column I. This oral identification of words ought to be timed.

COLUMN I	COLUMN II	COLUMN III
1. **arrive**	a. come	a. leave
	b. depart	b. run
	c. begin	c. reach
2. **assemble**	a. disperse	a. show
	b. gather	b. point
	c. get to	c. scatter
3. **be able**	a. be capable	a. be incapable
	b. cannot	b. can
	c. unable	c. scatter
4. **begin**	a. start	a. stay
	b. leave	b. end
	c. terminate	c. continue

5. **come**
   a. study
   b. arrive
   c. go

   a. start
   b. commence
   c. leave

6. **different**
   a. distinct
   b. new
   c. happy

   a. similar
   b. dissimilar
   c. interesting

7. **eager**
   a. capable
   b. competent
   c. anxious

   a. indifferent
   b. lounging
   c. happy

8. **early**
   a. happily
   b. at an early hour
   c. eagerly

   a. promptly
   b. late
   c. unhappy

9. **funny**
   a. happy
   b. carefree
   c. strange

   a. common
   b. withdrawn
   c. unfriendly

10. **glad**
   a. slow
   b. happy
   c. unusual

   a. aware
   b. sad
   c. unaware

B. Pick the right expression. Complete the following sentences with the term that best fits the situation. Read aloud.

class	many	laugh
morning	relative	customs
listen	like	classmate
stand up	delay	expressway
often	show	relaxed
traffic	interesting	assemble

1. If a class meets early in the day, it is a _____ class.
2. When students get up to tell their names they _____.
3. A freeway is an _____.
4. Your fellow student is your _____.
5. To point out a place means to _____ a place.
6. A lesson that is fascinating is _____.
7. When students gather in the classroom they _____.
8. If you discuss tradition, you also talk about _____.
9. When you talk about cars, trucks, etc., you're talking about _____.
10. If you want to hear what the teacher says, you_____.

C. In the space on the left write the word (s) that would best fit the expression(s) in **bold print**. Make other necessary changes. Read aloud.

_____ 1. The students **gather** in the classroom.
_____ 2. The teacher is **detained**.
_____ 3. Mr. Preston **comes** late.
_____ 4. There is a traffic jam on the **expressway**.
_____ 5. The students are **enthusiastic** to begin.
_____ 6. The lesson **starts** with new words.
_____ 7. They are all good **pupils**.
_____ 8. Mr. Preston is the **instructor**.
_____ 9. They come from many **sections** of the earth.
_____ 10. They **get up** to tell their names.
_____ 11. His name is **strange**.
_____ 12. Gloria Nave **chuckles** all the time.
_____ 13. Marcel is **happy** to have many friends.
_____ 14. Marcel is **fond** of America.
_____ 15. They will **journey** together.
_____ 16. The teacher **points out** many places.
_____ 17. They find it **fascinating**.
_____ 18. Students **frequently** eat in the cafeteria.
_____ 19. They are **amicable** and respect the **different** customs.

VII. - *Concept Recognition*

Fill in the word (phrase) most fitting to express the CONCEPT of the sentence according to the narrative. Read the complete sentence aloud.

A. The students wait for their teacher because_____.
   1. they like him   3. he is late
   2. they have a class   4. they study English

B. Mr. Preston is delayed on his way to school because_____.
   1. he cannot sleep   3. he forgets
   2. of a traffic jam   4. his car breaks down

C. The students are eager to study English. They need to learn it because_____.
   1. English is funny   3. it is the language of the land
   2. Mr. Preston speaks English 4. Marcel learns it

D. They don't know each other by name because_____.
   1. they are not intelligent   3. they live in France
   2. they cannot pronounce   4. they come from many
                                     sections of the world

E. To tell their names the students_____.
   1. sit down   3. stand up
   2. laugh   4. are glad

F. Gloria and Arturo study English because_____.
   1. they sit down   3. they are able
   2. they study   4. they are new Americans

G. Because the students are not French, they cannot_____.
   1. pronounce Marcel's name   3. speak English
   2. go to France   4. plan their vacation

H. Marcel goes to France to_____.
1. see Mr. Preston   3. visit his relatives
2. learn English   4. eat at the cafeteria

I. His friends plan their vacation because they _____.
1. like to travel   3. see the map
2. are students   4. like Marcel

J. While Mr. Preston points out places on the map, the students_____.
1. laugh   3. are glad
2. think it is funny   4. get acquainted

K. The students go to the cafeteria_____.
1. to eat and talk   3. to laugh
2. to look at the map   4. to learn the lesson

L. The cafeteria has_____.
1. many friends   3. a relaxed atmosphere
2. maps   4. many students

M. You learn about many things when you_____.
1. listen well   3. talk a lot
2. speak English   4. laugh

VIII. Telling the Meaning

A. Place a check mark (✔) in front of the word in Column II that best fits the MEANING of the word in Column I. Read aloud a complete sentence using this word.

COLUMN I   COLUMN II
1. **a lot of**   _____ a. few
                           _____ b. many
                           _____ c. great

2. **be acquainted with**
   _____ a. know
   _____ b. be ignorant of
   _____ c. be good

3. **be fond of**
   _____ a. dislike
   _____ b. correct
   _____ c. like

4. **chuckle**
   _____ a. cry
   _____ b. laugh
   _____ c. run

5. **come**
   _____ a. arrive
   _____ b. go
   _____ c. depart

6. **competent**
   _____ a. able
   _____ b. funny
   _____ c. unable

7. **detain**
   _____ a. hasten
   _____ b. delay
   _____ c. block

8. **fascinating**
   _____ a. interesting
   _____ b. boring
   _____ c. intelligent

9. **frequently**
   _____ a. seldom
   _____ b. quickly
   _____ c. often

10. **gather**
    _____ a. scatter
    _____ b. come
    _____ c. assemble

B. Pick the right expression.

1. Which word in paragraph A. means "near the beginning"? _____
2. Which word in paragraph A. means "not on time"? _____
3. Which word in paragraph C. means "strange"? _____
4. Which word in paragraph D. means "to go to see"? _____
5. Which word in paragraph E. means "point out"? _____
6. Which word in paragraph F. means "comfortable"? _____

C. Return to Exercise A. Place two check marks (✔✔) in front of the word in Column II that is the ATONYM of the word in Column I. Read aloud a complete sentence using this word.

D. Select one of the three (3) words (phrases) that best fulfills the MEANING of the sentence according to the narrative. Insert the word in the blank space. Read the complete sentence aloud.

1. Students gather in the classroom_____ in the morning.
   a. early   b. late   c. enthusiastically

2. The teacher is delayed, and he is _____ for class.
   a. prompt   b. late   c. early

3. There is a traffic jam which _____ him.
   a. detains   b. hastens   c. waits

4. When Mr. Preston comes to class, the students are _____ to learn English.
   a. idle   b. eager   c. intelligent

5. To live in America, the students _____ to learn English.
   a. want   b. arrive   c. place

6. The students _____ and tell their names.
   a. sit down   b. get up   c. depart

7. Gloria and Arturo are Americans, but Marcel _____ from Paris, France.
   a. goes   b. thinks   c. comes

8. Gloria thinks Marcel has a _____ name.
   a. serious   b. able   c. strange

9. The students are _____ to pronounce the name.
   a. able   b. sad   c. strange

10. Marcel is _____ to be in the United States.
    a. sad   b. glad   c. envious

11. He is_____ his American friends.
    a. fond of   b. happy of   c. glad of

12. Mr. Preston and Marcel _____ some places on the map.
    a. hide   b. show   c. go

13. The places are_____ and the students are _____ to visit them.
    a. fascinating, eager   b. boring, idle   c. serious, unable

14. After school the students _____ meet in the _____.
    a. seldom, school   b. frequently, restaurant   c. travel, home

15. People have _____, but they are _____.
    a. same air, unfriendly   b. different customs, friendly   c. tense world, keen

IX. Comprehension Exercises

A. Place a check mark (✔) in front of the correct answer to each of the questions according to the narrative. Do not consult the narrative. Read the complete sentences aloud.

1. When do the students meet for class?
   _____ a. When the teacher arrives.
   _____ b. Early in the morning.
   _____ c. When the time comes.

2. Who is late for class?
   _____ a. Mr. Preston is late for class.
   _____ b. The students are late for class.
   _____ c. Marcel is late for class.

3. Why is Mr. Preston delayed?
   _____ a. Because he waits for the students.
   _____ b. Because he cannot find the way.
   _____ c. Because there is a traffic jam on the freeway.

4. Where do the students come from?
   _____ a. They come from France.
   _____ b. They come from the United States.
   _____ c. They come from many parts of the world.

5. What does Mr. Preston tell the students?
   _____ a. He tells them to sit down.
   _____ b. He tells them to stand up.
   _____ c. He tells them to read.

6. What does Gloria think about Marcel?
   _____ a. She thinks he is sad.
   _____ b. She thinks he has a funny name.
   _____ c. She thinks he is serious.

7. Where does Mr. Preston point out places?
    _____ a. He points them out on the map.
    _____ b. He points them out in the book.
    _____ c. He points them out in the cafeteria.

8. How is the lesson?
    _____ a. The lesson is boring.
    _____ b. The lesson is fascinating.
    _____ c. The lesson is long.

9. Where do the students go after the lesson?
    _____ a. They go to the cafeteria.
    _____ b. They go home.
    _____ c. They travel.

10. Why do the students meet in the cafeteria?
    _____ a. They study.
    _____ b. They laugh.
    _____ c. Because it has a relaxed atmosphere.

11. What do the students do while they eat?
    _____ a. They sing.
    _____ b. They talk.
    _____ c. They play.

12. Why do some students listen?
    _____ a. Because they laugh.
    _____ b. Because they think.
    _____ c. Because they learn about things.

13. What do the students talk about?
    _____ a. About English.
    _____ b. About the United States.
    _____ c. About customs.

14. What do people have?

_____ a. They have different students.

_____ b. They have different customs.

_____ c. They have different friends.

B. Below there are three (3) different thoughts expressed in each of the exercises. Assign the proper sequence (order) of THOUGHT, according to the narrative, by numbering 1 to 3. Read aloud.

1. a. the teacher _____
   b. wait for _____
   c. the students _____

2. a. to begin their lesson _____
   b. the students _____
   c. are eager _____

3. a. each other _____
   b. they don't know _____
   c. by name _____

4. a. as they tell their names _____
   b. Mr. Preston tells the students _____
   c. to stand up _____

5. a. Marcel has _____
   b. Gloria thinks _____
   c. a funny name _____

6. a. Marcel has _____
   b. in France _____
   c. many relatives _____

7. a. to visit _____
   b. Marcel points out places _____
   c. on the map of France _____

8. a. the students go   _____
   b. after the lesson   _____
   c. to the cafeteria   _____

9. a. you can learn   _____
   b. when you listen well   _____
   c. about many things   _____

10. a. people have   _____
    b. but they are friendly   _____
    c. different customs   _____

C. There are some statements listed below about the narrative. Write **T** for **True** in front of each statement that you think is true. Write **F** for **False** if the statement is not true. Read aloud.

_____ 1. It is a late morning for class.
_____ 2. The students wait for Mr. Preston.
_____ 3. The teacher is delayed.
_____ 4. A traffic jam detained him.
_____ 5. The students are eager about learning.
_____ 6. The teacher tells them to stand up.
_____ 7. They tell their names after they stand up.
_____ 8. Gloria thinks Marcel has a sad name.
_____ 9. The students are sad.
_____ 10. Marcel plans his vacation early.
_____ 11. Mr. Preston shows places on the map.
_____ 12. The lesson is fascinating.
_____ 13. The students eat and talk in the cafeteria.
_____ 14. There is a relaxed atmosphere in the cafeteria.
_____ 15. When you listen, you learn.
_____ 16. The students talk about customs.
_____ 17. People have the same customs.
_____ 18. People are friendly.
_____ 19. Marcel likes his friends in America.

X. Composition and Discussion

A. In Column I are the beginnings of sentences. In Column II are the Completions to the sentences of Column I. Select the completion best fitting each sentence in Column I according to the narrative. Read the completed sentences orally. Compose new sentences orally and discuss the narrative.

Column I		Column II
1. The students assemble	a.	they just listen.
2. The students wait	b.	but they are friendly.
3. Mr. Preston is	c.	know each other by name.
4. Mr. Preston is delayed	d.	many parts of the world
5. There is a traffic jam	e.	to begin their lesson.
6. The teacher arrives	f.	the language of the land.
7. The students are eager	g.	five minutes later.
8. The students need to learn	h.	on the freeway.
9. The students don't	i.	on his way to school.
10. They come from	j.	late for class.
11. Gloria thinks Marcel	k.	in the classroom.
12. The students are unable	l.	for their teacher.
13. Marcel likes	m.	cafeteria after the lesson.
14. The students eat in the	n.	his American friends.
15. Some students don't talk	o.	to pronounce his name.
16. People have different customs	p.	has a funny name.

B.   1. Tell us about your English class.

2. Tell us about your friends in class and at home.

3. Describe a classroom scene in your hometown.

4. Tell about places on the map you are familiar with.

C. Read the poem aloud. Answer orally the questions listed following the poem.

Whispers of the Ages

There are whispers [1]   [1] soft voice sounds
In the mountains.
Do you hear them?

There are whispers of
The ages,[2] telling   [2] times
Tales,[3] can you hear?   [3] stories

There are whispers
Whispering tales
of many sages. [4]   [4] wise men

Can you hear?
Can you fathom [5]   [5] understanding
All the wisdom [6] *of the ages?*   [6] learning, knowledge

1. Identify the *nouns* and *determiners* in this poem.
2. Identify the *verbs* in this poem.
3. Identify *declarative* sentences in simple present tense.
4. What is the title of this poem?
5. Which word recurs most frequently?
6. What is the *main idea* of the poem?
7. Do you like the poem? Don't you like it? Why?

D. Describe what you see in the picture below.

CHAPTER TWO

A Weekend in the Country

IN THIS CHAPTER

Words to remember:
Present continuous tense

Adverbials of time:
*Saturday morning, every weekend,
minutes later, moments later, etc.*

Adverbials of frequency
Usually, sometimes, always, never, etc.

Words that describe (adjectives):
*Yellow, green, orange, black, etc.
Good, modest, small, hilly, wet, trembling, happy, etc.*

I. Narrative

A. The Campbells are a *typical* American family. Mr. Campbell is a lawyer. He *works* in Houston, Texas. He is a good lawyer. Mrs. Campbell is a housewife. She likes what she does; her husband, the *attorney*, likes his work too.

B. The Campbells own an inexpensive cabin in La Grange, Texas. La Grange is a small town of one hundred and five *miles* from Houston. The *countryside* is hilly, and the Colorado River runs through the *town*. The beauty of the countryside makes up for the discomfort of the living quarters.

C. The Campbells are *preparing* for a weekend in their country home. Mrs. Campbell buys groceries at the supermarket. Tim and Ann help their mother. Tim is eight years old and a third grader. Anne is in *junior high* school. She is fourteen years old. Together the two children get up early Saturday morning. They are making *sandwiches* for the family. Mike and Lucy usually help their father with the other chores. At the age of sixteen, Mike is the oldest child in the family. Lucy is the youngest in the family. She is only six years old.

---

typical: normal
works: is employed
attorney: lawyer
mile: 1.6 kilometers
countryside: rural region (area)
town: small city
preparing: making ready
junior high: middle school
sandwich: slices of bread with a
   filling of meat or cheese, etc.

stretch: extend the body to relax
river: a stream of water
ride: float on water
paddle: move the canoe
overturn: turn upside down, tip over
dive: plunge, jump head first
dripping: soaked
ground: place
concern: worry
marshmallows: soft candy

D. There are many rest areas on the highway. The Campbells sometimes stop to *stretch*. It's only a short distance to La Grange and they are eager to get there. There is a camping area near the *river*. People are always coming out to the river. There are boats and canoes for rent.

E. "I'd like a canoe *ride*," Lucy says. Mike takes her for a canoe ride. "Sit still while I *paddle*," he tells her, "or else the canoe can *overturn*." "I always behave don't I, Mike?" Lucy is smiling and Mike knows he cannot be cross with her.

F. Twenty minutes later, the canoe is tossed by the rapids. Not far down the river are the falls. Mike wants to turn back, but the rapids carry the canoe towards the falls. Many canoes overturn there. He yells for help. Lucy is not a good swimmer. Mike is afraid she might drown.

G. Soon, Mike loses control and the canoe tips over. "Hold on!" Mike yells at Lucy. But she cannot hear him. She is being dragged down toward the foaming falls. "My God! What can I do?" Mike thinks desperately. He feels helpless.

H. Sudenly a state trooper appears near the falls. Without hesitation, the officer *dives* into the water. Moments later, he is carrying little Lucy toward the place on shore where Mike is waiting.

I. *Dripping* wet and trembling under the trooper's blanket, the two young Campbells are brought to the picnic *grounds*. "Thank you, officer!" Mrs. Campbell exclaims. "We worried so when they were late for supper," she adds with *concern*.

J. "Not at all," the trooper responds. "Next time you must study the rapids before you get down that far." Everyone is happy now that Lucy and Mike are safe. They are sitting by the fire warming themselves and toasting *marshmallows*. Lucy is smiling again.

Idea Questions:

1. Where do the Campbells live?
2. Why do the Campbells spend their weekends in the country?
3. Why do some of the people like (not like) camping?
4. Where do people stop to rest on the highways?
5. Why do the Campbells want to stretch?
6. What danger is there in riding a canoe?
7. How does the canoe overturn?
8. Who comes to save Lucy?
9. Why do the young Campbells tremble under the blanket?
10. What about the MAIN IDEA in paragraph "J"?

II. Words in Context [Pictographs]

Below are words used in the narrative. Where possible, each word has a [synonym], or it is defined as used in the story. Where possible, an *(antonym)* is also given. Make up sentences about the pictographs choosing the words you need. Read aloud.

Example: [lawyer] = Mr. Campbell is a lawyer in Huston.

A. and B.

Typical [**normal**] *(unusual)*; attorney [**lawyer**]; law [**rule**] *(disorder)*; housewife [**married woman in charge of a household**] *(career woman)*; occupation [**line of work**] *(leisure)*; own [**possess**] *(lack)*; inexpensive [**simple**] *(ostentatious)*; cabin [**cottage**] *(mansion)*; countryside [**rural area**] *(municipality)*; hilly [**uneven terrain**] *(flat land)*; run [**flow**] *(stand still)*; make up [**compensate**] *(lack)*; discomfort [**annoyance**] *(contentment)*; living quarters [**residence**]

Drawing of paragraphs A & B

C. and D.

groceries [**food**]; supermarket [**grocery store**]; chore [**task**]; rest [**relax**] *(work)*; area [**spot**]; stop [**halt**] *(go)*; short [**small**] *(long)*; distance [**remoteness**] *(closeness)*; camping [**outing**]; near [**close**] *(distant)* weekend [**Saturday and Sunday**] *(weekday)*; boat [**vessel**]; canoe [**rowboat**]; rent [**pay for the use of**]

E. and F.

ride [**float on water**]; be still [**at rest**] *(be active)*; behave [**obey**] *(misbehave)*; smile [**grin**] *(frown)*; cross [**angry**] *(happy)*; minute [**moment**]; toss [**fling**]; rapids [**rushing water**]; falls [**falling water**]; turn back [**turn from**]; yell [**shout**] *(whisper)*; swim [**stay afloat**] *(sink)*; afraid [**frightened**] *(unafraid)*; drown [**sink**] *(stay afloat)*

Drawing of paragraphs C & D

G. and H.

lose [**fail to keep**] *(gain)*; control *(balance)*; tip over [**overturn**] *(stay upright)*; hold on [**grip**] *(let go)*; hear [**listen**] *(be deaf)*; drag [pull]; foam [**froth**]; desperately [**hopelessly**] *(hopefully)*; suddenly [**abruptly**] *(slowly)*; appear [**become visible**] *(disappear)*; hesitation [**pause**] *(haste)*; officer [**official**]; dive [**plunge**]; shore [**bank**]

I and J.

wet [**moist**] *(dry)* ; tremble [**shake**] *(be still)* ; under [**beneath**] *(on top)*; blanket [**covering**] ; young [**youthful**] *(old)* ; bring [**fetch**] *(send)* ; picnic [**outing**] ; exclaim [**cry out**] *(be silent)* ; worry [**concern**] *(unconcern)* ; late [**delayed**] *(early)* ; supper [**evening meal**] *(breakfast)* ; respond [**answer**] *(ignore)*; before [**prior to**] *(after)* ; safe [**out of danger**]; toast [**fry**]

Drawing of paragraphs E & F

III. Structures [Phrases]

Below are some phrases taken from the narrative. Make complete sentences and read them aloud.

1. a	good	attorney
2. a	modest	cabin
3. of	the	living quarters
4. for	a weekend	
5. at	the	supermarket
6. early	Saturday	morning
7. on	the	highway
8. out	to	the river
9. for	a	canoe ride
10. toward	the	falls

Drawing of paragraphs G & H

IV. Sentences

A. Read the following sentences aloud. Repeat, substituting, where possible, the synonym of the word in *italics* or a phrase which explains the meaning. Make other necessary changes.

Example: They own a *cabin*.   They own a *cottage*.

1. Mr. Campbell is an *attorney*.
2. Mrs. Campbell is a *housewife*.
3. She likes her *occupation*.
4. The countryside is *hilly*.
5. A river *runs* through the town.
6. They buy groceries at the *supermarket*.

Drawing of paragraphs I & J

7. There are many rest *areas* on the highway.
8. It's only a *short* distance.
9. The *rapids* carry them toward the falls.
10. Lucy is being *dragged* down the river.
11. He carries Lucy to the *shore*.
12. The Campbells are *concerned* about Lucy and Mike.

B. Fill the blanks with the words from the narrative. Each space may be filled by a word or phrase. Do not refer back to the narrative. Where possible, use variations of the missing words. Read aloud.

The Campbells are a_____ American _____. Mr. Campbell is a _____.
He_____ as a lawyer. Mrs. Campbell is a _____. She _____ what she does.

The Campbells _____ an _____ cabin. The countryside in La Grange is for the _____ of the _____ quarters.

The Campbells are _____ for a _____ in their _____ home. Mrs. Campbell buys _____ at the _____. Tim is eight _____ old. Ann is in _____ school. They get up early _____ morning. They are _____ sandwiches.

There are many _____ areas on the _____. The Campbells stop to _____. It's only a _____ _____ to La Grange. They are _____ to get there. The camping area is _____ the _____. There are _____ and _____ for _____.

Mike takes _____ for a _____ ride. She sits _____ while he _____. Mike can't be _____ at Lucy.

The canoe is _____ by the _____. The falls are not _____ down the _____. Mike wants to _____ back. The rapids _____ the _____ towards the_____. Many canoes _____ there. Mike _____ for _____. Lucy is not a _____ swimmer. Mike is _____ she might _____.

Soon Mike _____ control. The canoe _____ _____. "Hold _____!" Mike _____ at Lucy. She cannot _____ _____ him. She is being _____ down toward the _____ falls. "What will I _____mother and _____?" Mike thinks_____.

Suddenly, a _____ trooper _____ near the _____. Without _____, the _____ dives into the _____. Moments _____, he is _____ Lucy_____ the place_____.

_____ wet and _____ under the blanket, the two _____ Campbells are being _____ to the picnic_____. "Thank you, _____!" Mrs. Campbell _____.

"Not at _____,"the trooper _____. Everyone is _____ now that Lucy and Mike are _____. They are _____ at the fire _____ themselves and _____ Lucy is _____ again.

V. Grammar (Points of Interest)

A. The **Present Continuous Tense** expresses action in the PRESENT TIME. It is like the SIMPLE PRESENT TENSE, the NOW TENSE.

$$\text{Equation: } \begin{array}{l} \text{am} \\ \text{is} \\ \text{Are} \end{array} + \text{verb} + \text{ing}$$

PRESENT	PRESENT CONTINUOUS
He practices law.	He is practicing law.
They prepare for a weekend in the country.	They are preparing for a weekend in the country.
Mrs. Campbell buys groceries	Mrs. Campbell is buying groceries
Tim and Ann help their mother.	Tim and Ann are helping their mother.
They make sandwiches.	They are making sandwiches.
People come out to the river.	People are coming out to the river.
Mike thinks desperately.	Mike is thinking desperately.
They sit by the fire.	They are sitting by the fire.

B. 1. **Adverbials** of **time** answer the question **when?**

> They get up early *Saturday morning.*
> The Campbells go to La Grange *every weekend.*
> *Twenty minutes later*, he is carrying Lucy to shore.

2. **Adverbials** of **frequency** answer the question **how often?**

> Mike and Lucy *usually* help their father.
> The Campbells *sometimes* stop to stretch.
> People are *always* coming out to the river.
> He knows that he can *never* be cross at Lucy.

C. Words that describe (**Adjectives**) are:

1. Colors: yellow   orange   green   black, etc.

or

2. Words such as

good	He is a *good* attorney
modest	They own a *modest* cabin.
small	La Grange is a *small* town.
hilly	The countryside is *hilly*
wet	She is *wet* and trembling.
trembling	She was frightened and *trembling*.
happy	They are *happy* now.

VI. Word Recognition

A. Circle the word(s) in Column II most *like* the word in Column I, and the word(s) in Column III most *unlike* the word in Column I. This oral identification of words ought to be timed.

COLUMN I	COLUMN II	COLUMN III
1. **afraid**	a. cross b. frightened c. pleased	a. unafraid b. angry c. happy
2. **behave**	a. be at rest b. smile c. obey	a. misbehave b. be active c. yell
3. **buy**	a. stop b. purchase c. rest	a. hinder b. work c. sell
4. **cabin**	a. small house b. river c. picnic	a. stream b. countryside c. mansion
5. **desperately**	a. hopelessly b. suddenly c. abruptly	a. hopefully b. slowly c. hesitantly
6. **discomfort**	a. fear b. uneven terrain c. annoyance	a. order b. contentment c. cabin
7. **flow**	a. practice b. yell c. run	a. stand still b. lack c. go
8. **hear**	a. yell b. shout c. listen	a. whisper b. be deaf c. sink

9. **help**

   a. pass
   b. wait
   c. assist

   a. hinder
   b. relax
   c. hold on

10. **hesitation**

    a. leisure
    b. pause
    c. fun

    a. hopelessness
    b. desperation
    c. haste

11. **hilly**

    a. modest
    b. uneven terrain
    c. distant

    a. big
    b. flat
    c. small

12. **hold on**

    a. behave
    b. grip
    c. regulate

    a. let go
    b. tip over
    c. overturn

13. **late**

    a. under
    b. delayed
    c. below

    a. on top
    b. above
    c. early

14. **law**

    a. occupation
    b. rule
    c. chore

    a. practice
    b. career
    c. disorder

15. **lose**

    a. control
    b. regulate
    c. fail to keep

    a. tip over
    b. gain
    c. overturn

16. **modest**

    a. married
    b. normal
    c. inexpensive

    a. happy
    b. ostentatious
    c. nice

17. **occupation**

    a. line of work
    b. hobby
    c. boat

    a. work
    b. leisure
    c. smile

18. **own**

a. stop
b. possess
c. help

a. hinder
b. sell
c. lack

19. **rest**

a. run
b. relax
c. ride

a. sell
b. work
c. buy

20. **safe**

a. warm
b. hot
c. protected

a. unsafe
b. cold
c. far

B. Recognize words in the Narrative.

1. Which word in paragraph A. means that the Campbell's are a "normal" family?

2. Which word in paragraph B. means "modest"?

3. Which word in paragraph C. means that the Campbells are "making ready" for the weekend?

4. Which word in paragraph D. means "outing"?

5. Which word in paragraph E. means that the Campbells are "looking forward to" getting there?

6. Which word in paragraph F. means that the canoes "tip over"?

7. Which word in paragraph G. means that Lucy is being "pulled" down the river?

8. Which word in paragraph H. means that a trooper appears "abruptly"?

9. Which word in paragraph I. means that Lucy is "dripping wet"?

10. Which word in paragraph J. means "prior to"?

C. In the space on the left, write the word(s) that would best fit the expression in **bold print**. Make other necessary changes. Read aloud.

_____ 1. The Campbells are a **normal** family.

_____ 2. Mr. Campbell is an **attorney**.

_____ 3. They **possess** a cabin in La Grange.

_____ 4. The cabin is **simple**.

_____ 5. They like visiting the **rural** area.

_____ 6. The beauty **compensates** for the discomfort.

_____ 7. They **purchase** groceries.

_____ 8. The children prepare for the **outing**.

_____ 9. They **assist** their Mother.

_____ 10. The Campbells **relax** at the picnic.

_____ 11. The **region** has a river.

_____ 12. Mrs. Campbell buys groceries at the **supermarket**.

_____ 13. There are **vessels** at the river.

_____ 14. They **pay for the use of** a canoe.

_____ 15. There are rest **spots** on the highway.

_____ 16. The Campbells **halt** to stretch.

_____ 17. Mike cannot be **grumpy**.

_____ 18. He **grins** at Lucy.

_____ 19. **Moments** later there are the falls.

_____ 20. The rapids **transport** the boat.

_____ 21. They **yell** for help.

_____ 22. Mike is **afraid** Lucy might drown.

_____ 23. She tries **hopelessly** to keep afloat.

_____ 24. Mrs. Campbell worries when they are **delayed**.

_____ 25. They sit **protected** near the fireplace.

VII. Concept Recognition

Fill in the most appropriate word (phrase) to express the concept of the sentence according to the narrative. Read the complete sentence aloud.

A. The Campbells go to La Grange to _____.
1. relax
3. work
2. ride
4. drive

B. The beauty makes up for the _____.
1. ride
3. discomfort
2. rover
4. rest area

C. The Campbells buy groceries to _____.
1. take home
3. see the countryside
2. prepare for the weekend.
4. take a boat ride

D. Tim and Ann get up early Saturday to_____.
1. go to school
3. drive to La Grange
2. help their father
4. make sandwiches

E. The Campbells stop on the highway to_____.
1. stretch
3. eat
2. study
4. read

F. People are always coming out to the river because _____.
1. there are blankets
3. eat
2. there are people
4. read

G. Mike tells Lucy to sit still because _____.
1. he likes her
3. she smiles
2. the canoe can overturn
4. the family waits

H. Lucy is smiling and Mike knows _____.
1. the boat will tip
3. he swims well
2. Mother is waiting
4. he cannot be cross with her

I. Mike yells for help because _____.
   1. Lucy is not a good swimmer   3. the falls are near
   2. he sees the trooper   4. he sees his father

J. Lucy cannot hear Mike because _____.
   1. she swims away   3. she is on the shore
   2. she is being dragged down   4. the trooper is helping
      towards the falls

K. The trooper dives into the water to_____.
   1. swim   3. relax
   2. help Lucy   4. help Mike

L. The two young Campbells are trembling because_____.
   1. they are dripping wet   3. they are under the blanket
   2. they are at home   4. they are toasting marshmallows

M. Mrs. Campbell was worried_____.
   1. when Lucy and Mike return   3. when Lucy and Mike
                             were late for supper
   2. when the trooper came   4. when Mr. Campbell yells

N. Before they go down far on the river_____.
   1. they must rent a canoe   3. they must study the rapids
   2. they must tell Mrs. Campbell   4. they must tell no one

O. Everyone is happy because_____.
   1. Mrs. Campbell is worried   3. the trooper comes
   2. Lucy and Mike are safe   4. the blanket is warm

P. Lucy is smiling as she_____.
   1. sits by the fire   3. talks to Ann
   2. eats a sandwich   4. swims in the rapids

VIII. Telling the Meaning

A. Place a check mark (✔) in front of the word in Column II that best fits the MEANING of the word in Column I. Read aloud a complete sentence using this word.

COLUMN I   COLUMN II

1. **add**
   _____ a. subtract
   _____ b. respond
   _____ c. increase

2. **be still**
   _____ a. at rest
   _____ b. be active
   _____ c. be happy

3. **countryside**
   _____ a. municipality
   _____ b. cabin
   _____ c. rural area

4. **cross**
   _____ a. happy
   _____ b. angry
   _____ c. smile

5. **discomfort**
   _____ a. law
   _____ b. contentment
   _____ c. annoyance

6. **fail to keep**
   _____ a. lose
   _____ b. gain
   _____ c. hold on

7. **frightened**
   _____ a. glad
   _____ b. unafraid
   _____ c. afraid

8. **ground**

_____ a. water
_____ b. earth
_____ c. picnic

9. **help**

_____ a. hinder
_____ b. assist
_____ c. flow

10. **hopelessly**

_____ a. suddenly
_____ b. desperately
_____ c. hopefully

11. **make up**

_____ a. lack
_____ b. sink
_____ c. compensate

12. **moist**

_____ a. dry
_____ b. wet
_____ c. young

13. **near**

_____ a. close
_____ b. distant
_____ c. short

14. **possess**

_____ a. want
_____ b. lose
_____ c. own

15. **profession**

_____ a. discomfort
_____ b. occupation
_____ c. leisure

B. Pick the right expression. Complete the following sentences with the term that best fits the situation. Read aloud.

stretch	supermarket	ride
ground	uneven terrain	inexpensive
concern	paddle	dive
countryside	yell	typical
sandwich	preparing	overturn
relax	short	turn back

1. If you're driving though a rural area, you see the_____.

2. When you buy groceries, you do it in the_____.

3. If the countryside is hilly, the terrain is_____.

4. A family that is usual is_____.

5. You stop at the rest area to_____.

6. To ride a canoe, you have to_____.

7. Because the cabin is small, it is_____.

8. If you plunge into the river, you into the river. _____.

9. When you are scared, you for help. _____.

10. When you ride the canoe too close to the falls, it is too late to_____.

C. Return to Exercise A. Place two check marks (✔ ✔)in front of the word COLUMN II that is the ANTONYM of the word in COLUMN I. Read aloud a complete sentence using this word.

D. Select one of the three (3) words (phrases) that best fulfills the MEANING of the sentence according to the narrative. Insert the word in the blank space. Read the completed sentence aloud.

1. The Campbells go the La Grange to take a _____.
   a. rest   b. boat   c. canoe

2. They are not comfortable because the cabin is_____.
   a. hilly   b. small   c. typical

3. Mr. Campbell practices law. He is an_____.
   a. housewife   b. attorney   c. trooper

4. A cabin is usually a small house in the _____.
   a. municipality   b. countryside   c. residence

5. The countryside and the river_____ for the discomfort of the living quarters.
   a. compensate   b. lose   c. own

6. One of the chores in preparing for the picnic is_____.
   a. renting a boat   b. buying groceries   c. relaxing

7. The Campbells stop on the highway to _____.
   a. rnet   b. assist   c. stretch

8. People are always coming out to the river because _____.
   a. they buy groceries b. they live   c. they rent boats
                             in the city   and canoes

9. Lucy sits still. She's afraid the canoe can _____.
   a. stop   b. stand   c. overturn

10. When Lucy smiles, Mike knows he cannot be _____ with her.
    a. cross   b. happy   c. still

11. Mike loses _____ and the canoe tips over.
    a. hold   b. control   c. Lucy

12 The rapids drag Lucy towards the falls. She cannot _____ Mike.

a. hold on   b. lose   c. hear

13. The trooper dives into the river without _____ because Lucy is
_____.

a. hesitation,   b. haste, staying   c. a blanket, smiling
                             drowning   afloat

14. Mrs. Campbell is worried when the Campbells are _____
for the _____.

a. late, evening meal   b. absent, party   c. returned, river

15. The young Campbells tremble under the blanket because they are
_____.

a. cold   b. crisp   c. soft

16. Now the young Campbells are _____ everyone is _____.

a. far, unsafe   b. unsafe, warm   c. safe, warm

17. The fire is hot and they _____ marshmallows.

a. increase   b. toast   c. rent

18. Lucy is smiling because she's_____.

a. safe   b. hot   c. near

IX. Comprehension I Exercises]

A. Place a check mark (✔) in front of the correct answer to each
of the questions according to the narrative. Read the complete
sentence aloud.

1. Who are the Campbells?

_____ a. They are friends.

_____ b. They are a typical American family.

_____ c. They are smiling.

2. Who practices law?

_____ a. Mr. Campbell.

_____ b. Mrs. Campbell.

_____ c. Mike.

3. Does Mrs. Campbell like being a housewife?

_____ a. Yes, she does.

_____ b. No, she doesn't.

_____ c. She thinks about it.

4. Why do the Campbells go to La Grange?

_____ a. They like to swim.

_____ b. They like their occupation.

_____ c. They own a small cabin.

5. How far is it to La Grange from Houston?

_____ a. Two hundred miles.

_____ b. One hundred and five miles.

_____ c. Twenty-five miles.

6. The Colorado River flows through

_____ a. the town.

_____ b. the highway.

_____ c. Houston.

7. What are Tim and Ann preparing?

_____ a. They help with the chores.

_____ b. They are making sandwiches.

_____ c. They are renting a canoe.

8. Who is the youngest in the family?

_____ a. Tim.

_____ b. Lucy.

_____ c. Mike.

9. Where are the rest areas?

_____ a. In Houston.

_____ b. On the river.

_____ c. On the highway.

10. When do the Campbells go to La Grange?

_____ a. Every day.

_____ b. On Saturday and Sunday.

_____ c. On Wednesday.

11. Why do people come out to the river?

_____ a. There are many people.

_____ b. There is water.

_____ c. There are boats and canoes

12. Why must Lucy sit still?

_____ a. Because she is smiling.

_____ b. Because the canoe will overturn.

_____ c. Because Mike is afraid.

13. Why does Mike know he cannot be cross with Lucy?

_____ a. Because she is small.

_____ b. Because she is smiling.

_____ c. Because he is fifteen-years old.

14. How does the canoe tip over?

_____ a. The trooper dives in.

_____ b. Mike loses control.

_____ c. Lucy is frightened.

15. Why does Mike yell for help?

_____ a. Because Lucy is not a good swimmer.

_____ b. Because he sees a trooper.

_____ c. Because he is sad.

16. What does the trooper do?

_____ a. He yells.

_____ b. He dives into the water.

_____ c. He smiles.

17. Why do the young Campbells tremble?

_____ a. They are happy.

_____ b. They are cold.

_____ c. They are late.

18. What does the trooper say to the Campbells?

_____ a. They must swim.

_____ b. They must go to the cabin.

_____ c. They must study the rapids.

19. Why is everyone happy?

_____ a. Because they sit at the fire.

_____ b. Because Lucy and Mike are safe.

_____ c. Because they are toasting marshmallows.

B. Below are three (3) different thoughts expressed in each of the exercises. Assign the proper sequence (order) of THOUGHT, according to the narrative, by numbering 1 to 3. Read aloud.

1. a. in Houston, Texas _____

   b. and he works _____

   c. Mr. Campbell is a lawyer _____

2. a. is a housewife and _____

   b. Mrs. Campbell _____

   c. she likes her occupation _____

3. a. an inexpensive cabin in La Grange, _____

   b. Texas _____

   c. the Campbells own _____

4. a. the Colorado River _____
    b. the countryside is hilly, and _____
    c. flows through the town _____

5. a. one hundred and five _____
    b. La Grange is a small town _____
    c. miles from Houston _____

6. a. in their country home _____
    b. the Campbells are preparing _____
    c. for a weekend _____

7. a. at the supermarket _____
    b. buys groceries _____
    c. Mrs. Campbell _____

8. a. Saturday morning _____
    b. get up early _____
    c. together they _____

9. a. for the family _____
    b. making sandwiches _____
    c. they are _____

10. a. with other chores _____
    b. Mike and Lucy usually _____
    c. help their father _____

11. a. on the highway _____
    b. rest areas _____
    c. there are many _____

12. a. they are eager to get there _____
    b. it's only a short _____
    c. distance to La Grange and _____

13. a. coming out _____
    b. to the river _____
    c. people are always _____

14. . boats and canoes _____
    b. for rent _____
    c. there are _____

15. a. be cross with her _____
    b. Lucy is smiling and _____
    c. Mike knows he cannot _____

16. a. tossed by the rapids _____
    b. the canoe is _____
    c. twenty minutes later, _____

17. a. the canoe toward the falls _____
    b. but the rapids carry _____
    c. Mike wants to turn back, _____

18. a. the canoe tips over _____
    b. Mike loses control and _____
    c. soon _____

19. a. toward the foaming falls _____
    b. dragged down _____
    c. she is _____

20. a. near the falls _____
    b. a state trooper appears _____
    c. suddenly, _____

21. a. into the water _____
    b. the officer dives _____
    c. without hesitation _____

22. a. he is carrying Lucy toward   _____
    b. Mike is waiting   _____
    c. the place on shore where   _____

23. a. before you get down that far   _____
    b. study the rapids   _____
    c. next time you must   _____

24. a. now that Lucy   _____
    b. everyone is happy   _____
    c. and Mike are safe   _____

25. a. by the fire   _____
    b. toasting marshmallows   _____
    c. they are   _____

26. a. again   _____
    b. is smiling   _____
    c. Lucy   _____

C. There are some statements listed below about the narrative. Write
   T for **True** in front of each statement that you think is true. Write
   F for **False** if the statement is not true. Read aloud.

   _____ 1. The Campbells are a typical American family.

   _____ 2. Mr. Campbell practices law.

   _____ 3. Mrs. Campbell likes her occupation.

   _____ 4. The Campbells own a mansion in La Grange.

   _____ 5. The countryside is flat in La Grange.

   _____ 6. Their cabin is comfortable.

   _____ 7. The Campbells spend some weekends in La Grange.

   _____ 8. They get up late on Saturday.

_____ 9. Mike and Lucy usually help their father.

_____ 10. Mike is the youngest in the family.

_____ 11. There are many rest areas on the highway.

_____ 12. It's a long distance to La Grange.

_____ 13. There is a camping area near the river.

_____ 14. People never come to the river.

_____ 15. There are boats for rent.

_____ 16. Mike tells Lucy to sit still.

_____ 17. The canoe is overturned by the rapids.

_____ 18. The rapids transport the canoe in the direction of the waterfalls.

_____ 19. Mike shouts for help.

_____ 20. Lucy stays afloat.

_____ 21. Mike fails to keep control of the canoe.

_____ 22. Lucy is being dragged up the river.

_____ 23. The state trooper dives into the water.

_____ 24. Mrs. Campbell is thankful.

_____ 25. The young Campbells sit near the fire.

_____ 26. Everyone is happy now that they are safe.

X. Composition and Discussion

A. In Column I are beginnings of sentences. In Column II are the completions to the sentences of Column I. Select the completion best fitting each sentence in Column I according to the narrative. Read the completed sentences orally. Compose new sentences orally and discuss the narrative.

	Column I		Column II
1.	The Campbells are	a.	is a housewife.
2.	Mrs. Campbell	b.	a typical American family.
3.	The Campbells	c.	are safe.
4.	The countryside	d.	flows through the town.
5.	The Colorado River	e.	before you get down that far.
6.	The Campbells are preparing	f.	to the camping ground.
7.	They are making	g.	"Thank you, officer!"
8.	There are many	h.	smiling again.
9.	There is a camping area	i.	and toasting marshmallows.
10.	People are always	j.	owns an inexpensive cabin.
11.	Mike takes Lucy	k.	for a weekend in their country home.
12.	The trooper brings Lucy	l.	sandwiches for the family.
13.	Lucy and Mike are brought	m.	rest areas on the highway.
14.	Mrs. Campbell exclaims	n.	near the river.
15.	You must study the rapids	o.	for a canoe ride.
16.	Mike and Lucy	p.	safely to shore.
17.	They are sitting by the fire	q.	coming out of the river
18.	Lucy is	r.	so hilly.

B. 1. Tell us about your family
2. Describe a river you know
3. Describe the countryside where you live
4. Tell us about an outing you have gone on
5. Tell us about your home

C. Describe what you see in the picture below.

D. Read the poem aloud. Answer orally the question listed following the poem.

Hope

The hope [1] for better times to come	[1] a feeling that what is desired
is stronger than the will	will happen
to end the pain [2]	[2] hurt
at once [3]	[3] immediately
In quiet mediation [4] I spend	[4] contemplation, thought
my free moments in	
bitterness [5] end	[5] sadness
my thoughts.	
Nothing remains [6] but hope	[6] is left
that better times must come,	
if only the will [7] to	[7] desire
live is strong [8]	[8] powerful
enough...	

1. Identify the *adjectives* in this poem.

2. Identify the *main idea.*

3. What is the meaning of the third verse?

4. Which verse expresses optimism?

5. What idea is expressed in the last verse?

CHAPTER THREE

THE PHILANTHROPIST

IN THIS CHAPTER

Words to remember
Simple past tense
Past continuous

Indefinite pronouns:

every-	*-boy*
any-	*-one*
some-	*-thing*
no-	

Question words:
what? where? who? when? why? how?

Adjective	**Comparative**	**Superlative**
old	*older*	*oldest*

I. Narrative

A. Curtis Smith came from a *low income* family of nine. At the age of sixteen he was the second oldest child in the family. He came from the "wrong side of the tracks," as the saying goes. The house where he lived was overcrowded, but clean. The children helped with the *housekeeping*.

B. Now Curtis was in trouble. Mr. and Mrs. Smith called on Mr. Campbell to seek counsel. Curtis was a friend of Mike Campbell. He attended Mike's high school when the busing was ordered. The authorities *intended* to offer equal education opportunity to children of lower income *households*. This brought Mike and Curtis together. Both were on the *varsity* football team. They became friends quickly.

C. Mr. Campbell listened attentively. He made many *notes* which he intended to use in the court. He assured Mr. and Mrs. Smith that he was going to do all he could for Curtis. "Don't you worry, it isn't as bad as it *seems*." "The police were kind," Mrs. Smith said. "They allowed Curtis to *call* me." "That wasn't kindness, Mrs. Smith. The one phone call was his constitutional right," Mr. Campbell *assured* her.

---

hurt: little
income: earning
housekeeping: management of a house
intended: had in mind
household: family
varsity: the main team
notes: remarks
seems: appears, looks like
call: phone
assured: guaranteed

testified: gave evidence
steal: take without permission
belong: have a proper place
rapped: tapped
gavel: a wooden hammer
maintained: defended
oath: solemn promise to tell the truth
tackle: player in football
goods: property, merchandise
prosecuting: public official
circumstances: occurrences

D. The warehouse guards pointed accusing fingers at Curtis. They *testified* that he was the man who broke into the warehouse. Those present in the courtroom whispered: "Somebody ought do something about it!" "First they take over our schools, then they *steal* from us." "What's next?" "They should stay where they *belong*." The judge *rapped* his *gavel*. Curtis' friends and neighbors *maintained* his innocence. They declared under *oath* that he was a good boy, who never did wrong.

E. The judge was confused. The court must know beyond a reasonable doubt that a man is guilty. He cannot be convicted otherwise. The judge thought of a plan whereby everyone could benefit. A thorough investigation of Curtis' personal activities was ordered. The court recessed for one week.

F. When the court reconvened, the following was revealed by the investigation: When Curtis first came to Euclid High, his peers avoided him. Even when he was accepted as a *tackle* on the team, they did not treat him as an equal. They came from well-to-do families. He did not belong.

G. When the war broke out overseas, the team adopted an orphanage in a small town. Each month a contribution was sent there which helped to sustain the war victims. Curtis wanted to contribute. He began by breaking into small stores. The money which he received for the stolen *goods* went to the orphanage. He became one of the team.

H. "This was the reason why Curtis stole, your Honor," Mr. Campbell ended his plea. "We throw ourselves on the mercy of the court." The judge deliberated quietly with the *prosecuting* attorney. Moments later, the judge spoke.

I. "In view of the *circumstances*, we cannot take stern measures against the accused, Curtis Smith. We pass a suspended sentence, and place Curtis Smith in the custody of his parents."

Idea Questions:

1. Why did the authorities order busing?*
2. Why did Mrs. Smith seek counsel?
3. Why did the people whisper in the courtroom?
4. What is a constitutional right?
5. What must the court know?
6. Why did the court order an investigation?
7. Was it a good idea to send money to an orphanage?
8. What did you think about Curtis Smith?
9. Do you agree with the court's decision?
10. What is the MAIN IDEA in The Philanthropist?

II. Words in Context [Pictographs]

Below are some of the words used in the narrative. Where possible, each word has a [synonym]; or it is defined as used in the story. Where possible, and *(antonym)* is also given. Make up sentences about the pictograph choosing the words you need. Read aloud.

Example: [philanthropist]= This story tells about a philanthropist.

A. and B.

Philanthropist [humanitarian] *(misanthrope)* ; wrong side of the tracks [ill-bred] *(well-bred)* ; overcrowded [congested] *(spacious)*; clean [sanitary] *(dirty)* ; able [competent] *(unable)*; least [minimum] *(most)* ; deep [profound] *(shallow)*; trouble [distress] *(tranquility)* ; call on [visit] *(leave)* ; seek [look for] *(find)* ; counsel [advise] ; attend [be present] *(be absent)* ; busing* [transporting]; order [command]; authority [power]; offer [give] *(rescind)* ; equal [same] *(unequal)* ; low [small] *(high)* ; income [salary] ; together [jointly] *(separately)* ; team [group] *(individual)* ; quickly [rapidly] *(slowly)*

* In order to integrate schools, authorities ordered that students from one section of a town be transported to another. This was called "busing."

Drawing of paragraphs A & B

C. and D.

listen [**hear**] *(ignore)*; attentively [**closely**] *(negligently)* ; court [**tribunal**]; assure [**pledge**]; worse [**more unfavorable**] *(better)* ; kind [**sympathetic**] *(unkind)*; allow [**permit**] *(deny)*; constitutional [**inherent**]; right [**prerogative**]; warehouse [**storage building**]; guard [**sentry**]; point at [**single out**]; accusing [**incriminating**]; break into [**make illegal entry**]; testify [**witness**]; somebody [**someone**] *(nobody)*; something [**anything**] *(nothing)*; take over [**dominate**] *(give up)*; innocence [**lack of guilt**] *(guilt)*; declare [**advise**] *(stifle)*; wrong [**error**] *(right)*

Drawing of paragraphs C & D

E. and F.

confused [**perplexed**] *(orderly)*; beyond [**past**] *(near)*; reasonable [**rational**] *(unreasonable)*; doubt [**uncertainty**] *(certainty)*; guilty [**at fault**] *(innocent)*; convicted [**found guilty**] *(acquitted)*; benefit [**profit**] *(lose)*; thorough [**complete**] *(careless)*; investigation [**examination**]; personal [**private**] *(public)*; activity [**action**] *(inactivity)*; recess [**pause**] *(reconvene)*; reconvene [**meet again**] *(recess)*; follow [**succeed**] *(precede)*; reveal [**disclose**] *(cover up)*; first [**original**] *(last)*; peer [**equal**] *(unequal)*; avoid [**shun**] *(accept)*; consent [**approve**] *(reject)*; well-to-do [**rich**] *(poor)*

Drawing of paragraphs E & F

G. and H. and I.

war [**conflict**] *(peace)*; break out [**begin**] *(end)*; adopt [**support**] *(discard)*; orphanage [**institution for children without parents**]; contribute [**donate**] *(receive)*; victim [**prey**] *(aggressor)*; sustain [**support**] *(release)*; steal [**rob**] *(buy)*; plea [**request**]; mercy [**pity**] *(severity)*; deliberate [**consider**]; quietly [**silently**] *(noisily)*; circumstance [**occurrence**]; stern [**severe**] *(lenient)*; against [**opposed**] *(for)*; suspend [**dismiss**]; sentence [**judgment**] *(acquittal)*; place in custody [**legal guardianship**]

Drawing of paragraphs G, H & I

III. Structures (*Phrases*)

Below are some phrases taken from the narrative. Make complete sentences and read them aloud.

1.	the	- Curtis	- second	- family	- oldest
2.	from	- come	- the		- other side
3.	in	- be	- deep	- in	- trouble
4.	to	- come	- seek		- counsel
5.	of	- Curtis	- Mike Campbell	- friend	
6.	when	- authorities	- the	- order	- busing
7.	of	- be	- lower		- income
8.	who	- wrong	- never	- anything	- do
9.	that	- innocent	- a man	- proven	- is guilty
10.	for	- recess	- one	- court	- week
11.	him	- accept	- as		- an equal

IV. Sentences

A. Read the following sentences aloud. Repeat, substituting where possible, the synonym of the word in *italics*, or a phrase that explains the meaning. Make other necessary changes.

B. Fill in the blanks with words from the narrative. Each space may be filled by a word or phrase. Do not refer back to the narrative. Where possible, use variations of the missing words. Read aloud.

Curtis_____ from a_____ family. He _____ the second child. The house _____ he lived _____ overcrowded. The children _____ with the _____.

Curtis _____ in deep _____. He was a _____ of Mike. He _____ Mike's school. The busing _____ ordered.

The authorities _____ to offer equal _____. Mike and Curtis _____ on the varsity football_____. They _____ friends.

Mr. Campbell _____ attentively. He _____ many notes. He was gong to _____ them in _____. They _____ Curtis to _____. It was his _____ right.

The guards _____ accusing _____. They _____ that Curtis _____ into the warehouse. The judge _____ his gavel. The neighbors _____ his innocence. They_____ he was a_____ boy.

The judge was _____. A man must be _____ beyond _____ doubt. He can _____ be convicted_____. The _____ of a plan. An investigation was _____.

The_____ revealed that _____. At first his _____ avoided Curtis. They did not _____ him as an _____. They came from _____ families. He _____ not _____.

The team _____ an orphanage. A _____ was sent each _____. Curtis _____ to contribute. He _____ into small _____. He gave the _____ to the orphanage. He was one _____ team.

Mr. Campbell _____ his plea. The judge _____ silently. _____ later the _____ spoke. "We _____ a suspended _____." Curtis was _____ in the custody of his _____.

V. Grammar (Points of Interest)

A. **Simple Past Tense.** Regular verbs form their past tense by adding -ed or -d to the verb.

Example: attended   visited   called
             listened   assured   accused

Curtis *attended* Euclid High.
She *visited* Mr. Campbell.
She *called* on Mr. Campbell.
The authorities *intended* to offer equal education.
They *allowed* Curtis to call.

PAST TENSE is used to:

1. State facts about past conditions or events.
    The team *adopted* an orphanage.
    Mr. Campbell *assured* her.
    His neighbors *testified*.

2. Make general statements about a particular time.
    When the court *reconvened*, the following was revealed.
    Last year he was *accepted* as a tackle.
    Every month they *contributed* to the orphanage.

Some verbs have an irregular* pattern of the PAST TENSE.

PRESENT	PAST	
be	was	were
go	went	
do	did	
break	broke	
can	could	

Examples of past tense :

He *was* the second oldest.
Curtis never *did* wrong.
The war *broke* out overseas.

B. Past Continuous. The continuous form of the past tense expresses action still happening.

$$\text{Equation:} \quad \begin{matrix} was \\ were \end{matrix} \quad + \quad verb \quad + \quad \text{-}ing$$

PAST	PAST CONTINUOUS
The war *broke out.*	The war *was breaking out.*
He *broke into* the store.	He *was breaking into* a store.
They *contributed* to an orphanage.	They *were contributing* to an orphanage.

C. 1. Indefinite Pronouns refer to unknown persons, things, or indefinite quantities. The indefinite pronouns are the words in COLUMN I plus the words in COLUMN II.

I		II
every		
any-	+	*-body*
some-		*-one*
no-		*-thing*

*Can is a modal auxiliary.

Result

everybody	*everyone*	*everything*
anybody	*anyone*	*anything*
somebody	*someone*	*something*
nobody	*no one*	*nothing*

2. The indefinite form of the verb is the same form as we use with the pronoun, *he.**

   Somebody has to do something.
   Everyone points his finger at Curtis.
   Everybody enjoys football.

D. Question words are :

   1. *What*   was ordered?
   2. *Where***   are the people?
   3. *Who*   is accused of stealing?
   4. *When*   do they go to court?
   5. *Why* ***   are they accusing Curtis?
   6. *How*   can they say this?

E. Words that **Describe** or **Qualify** come in three (3) degrees :

   1. Adjective   A *good* friend is hard to find.
   2. Comparative   He is a *better* student than I.
   3. Superlative   Curtis was the second *oldest* child in the family.

To compare regular adjectives of one syllable we add -er, -est.
Adjectives of more than one syllable use the words more and most.

*Note: The verb form is that of the pronoun *he* (singular) because these
   words end in *-body*, *-one*, and *-thing*.
**Where needs the response *in*, *on*, or *at*. (*Where* is he? He's *in* court.)
***Why often needs the response *because*. (*Why* do the guards say that?
   Because they saw Curtis in the warehouse.)

   1. Adjective   He is an old friend.
   2. Comparative Mike is an older child than Ann.
   3. Superlative   He was the oldest child in the family.

F. Adjective [Relative] Clauses. The adjective clause generally modifies a preceding noun or a pronoun.

a time	*when*	He attended Mike's high school *when* busing was ordered.
a place	*where*	The house *where* he lived was clean.
a reason	*why*	This was the reason *why* Curtis stole.
a person	*who, whom or whose or that*	They declared *that* he was a goodboy *who* never did wrong.
a thing	*which or that*	The court must know *that* a man is guilty.

Note: The relative word where is sometimes used without denoting place (The judge thought of a plan whereby everyone could profit most.)

VI. Word Recognition

A. Circle the word(s) in Column II most *like* the word in Column I and the word(s) in Column III most *unlike* the word in Column I. This oral identification of words ought to be timed.

COLUMN I	COLUMN II	COLUMN III
1. **able**	a. adequate b. spacious c. clean	a. least b. unable c. inexpensive
2. **accept**	a. equal b. see c. approve	a. reject b. look c. meet

3. **against**
   - a. competent
   - b. opposed
   - c. with someone

   - a. lenient
   - b. for
   - c. considerate

4. **allow**
   - a. point at
   - b. permit
   - c. incriminate

   - a. deny
   - b. single out
   - c. accuse

5. **attend**
   - a. call
   - b. be present
   - c. advise

   - a. dispatch
   - b. deter
   - c. be absent

6. **benefit**
   - a. profit
   - b. work
   - c. complete

   - a. care
   - b. lose
   - c. earn

7. **call on**
   - a. seek
   - b. look for
   - c. visit

   - a. dispatch
   - b. find
   - c. leave

8. **confused**
   - a. perplexed
   - b. glad
   - c. happy

   - a. near
   - b. far
   - c. orderly

9. **declare**
   - a. ask
   - b. advise
   - c. seek

   - a. work
   - b. stifle
   - c. answer

10. **deep**
    - a. spacious
    - b. profound
    - c. least

    - a. congested
    - b. shallow
    - c. most

11. **doubt**
    - a. guilt
    - b. uncertainty
    - c. fault

    - a. certainty
    - b. innocence
    - c. acquittal

12. **follow**

    a. succeed
    b. cooperate
    c. disclose

    a. cover up
    b. avoid
    c. precede

13. **listen**

    a. believe
    b. hear
    c. say

    a. ignore
    b. answer
    c. assure

14. **parents**

    a. custody
    b. mother and father
    c. legal guardianship

    a. children
    b. orphanage
    c. judge

15. **philanthropist**

    a. well-bred person
    b. clean person
    c. humanitarian

    a. misanthrope
    b. lower class person
    c. duty person

16. **quietly**

    a. silently
    b. leniently
    c. suspended

    a. severely
    b. sternly
    c. noisily

B. Pick the right expression. Complete the following sentences with the term that best fits the situation. Read aloud.

deep	somebody	judgment
sentence	call on	victim
together	trouble	attend
against	least	mercy
benefit	worse	order
able	counsel	breaks in

1. When the judge makes a judgment he passes a_____.

2. If you profit from something, you can also say that you _____ from it.

3. When you do something jointly with someone, you are _____ with someone.

4. One who advises others is known to give_____.

5. To be present in a class means to _____ the class.

6. To fall prey to a thief is to become his_____.

7. When someone makes an illegal entry into a store he_____ _____.

8. Any time you are distressed you are in_____.

9. To have pity on someone means to have_____.

10. If you are opposed to war, you are _____ war.

C. In the space on the left write the word(s) that best fit the expression in **bold print.** Make the other necessary changes. Read aloud.

_____ 1. Curtis Smith was a **humanitarian.**

_____ 2. He was sixteen years of **age.**

_____ 3. Curtis came from the **lower class.**

_____ 4. The Smith house was **not spacious.**

_____ 5. But it **wasn't dirty.**

_____ 6. Mrs. Smith **visited** Mr. Campbell.

_____ 7. Curtis was in **profound** trouble.

_____ 8. Mr. Campbell gave his **advice.**

_____ 9. The authorities **commanded** busing.

_____ 10. They **gave** him equal education.

_____ 11. Mr. Campbell received a good **salary.**

_____ 12. Curtis was a member of a **group.**

_____ 13. He became Mike's friend **rapidly.**

_____ 14. The judge **heard** the witnesses.

_____ 15. He listened **closely.**

_____ 16. The court **pledged** justice.

_____ 17. The witnesses were **sympathetic.**

_____ 18. The court **permitted** a small recess.

_____ 19. This was Curtis' **inherent** right.

_____ 20. The neighbors **affirmed** his innocence.

_____ 21. Everyone was **perplexed.**

_____ 22. Everybody would **benefit.**
_____ 23. The court **met again** on the next day.
_____ 24. They heard Mr. Campbell's **request.**
_____ 25. The judge was **not severe.**

VII. Concept Recognition

Fill in the most appropriate word (phrase) to express the CONCEPT of the sentence according to the narrative. Read the complete sentence aloud.

A. Mrs. Smith came to Mr. Campbell to seek_____.
    1. counsel   3. Curtis
    2. Mike   4. her household

B. Curtis came from the _____ side of the tracks.
    1. good   3. wrong
    2. dirty   4. clean

C. Curtis attended Mike's high school because the busing was_____.
    1. summoned   3. dispatched
    2. ordered   4. trouble

D. The busing was commanded in order to offer _____ educational opportunity.
    1. deep   3. profound
    2. least   4. equal

E. Mike and Curtis were friends because they were on the same_____.
    1. authority   3. team
    2. expense   4. salary

F. The police allowed Curtis to call because it was_____.
    1. kindness   3. advice
    2. his constitutional right   4. his mother

G. Curtis was before the court because he was _____ of breaking into a _____.

1. permitted, school
3. accused, warehouse
2. tired, court
4. proud, tribunal

H. The court was confused because Curtis' neighbors _____ that he was a good boy.

1. declared
3. repressed
2. takeover
4. break into

I. The judge ordered an investigation whereby everyone would _____.

1. benefit
3. lose
2. recess
4. reveal

J. The investigation was to _____ the truth.

1. cover up
3. precede
2. reveal
4. follow

K. Curtis stole in order to _____ the money to the orphanage.

1. contribute
3. receive
2. plead
4. dismiss

VII. Telling the Meaning

Place a check mark (✔) in front of the word in COLUMN II that best fits the MEANING of the word in COLUMN I. Read aloud a complete sentence using this word.

COLUMN I	COLUMN II

1. advise
_____ a. right
_____ b. stifle
_____ c. declare

2. assure
_____ a. pledge
_____ b. better
_____ c. deny

3. be present   _____ a. attend
      _____ b. be absent
      _____ c. defer

4. beyond   _____ a. farther
      _____ b. near
      _____ c. most

5. contribute   _____ a. donate
      _____ b. receive
      _____ c. prey

6. distress   _____ a. counsel
      _____ b. tranquility
      _____ c. trouble

7. income   _____ a. expensive
      _____ b. salary
      _____ c. wealth

8. judgment   _____ a. dismissal
      _____ b. sentence
      _____ c. custody

9. listen   _____ a. hear
      _____ b. ignore
      _____ c. look

10. low   _____ a. high
      _____ b. small
      _____ c. custody

11. mother and father   _____ a. parents
      _____ b. children
      _____ c. legal guardianship

12. offer

_____ a. give

_____ b. rescind

_____ c. equal

13. overcrowded

_____ a. congested

_____ b. spacious

_____ c. clean

14. peer

_____ a. equal

_____ b. unequal

_____ c. well-to-do

15. permit

_____ a. do

_____ b. deny

_____ c. allow

16. perplexed

_____ a. confused

_____ b. orderly

_____ c. able

17. personal

_____ a. public

_____ b. private

_____ c. known

18. profound

_____ a. shallow

_____ b. deep

_____ c. least

B. Recognize words in the Narrative.

1. Which word in paragraph A. means "management of a house"?_____

2. Which word in paragraph B. means "had in mind"?_____

3. Which word in paragraph C. means "closely"?_____

4. Which word in paragraph D. means "make an illegal entry"?_____

5. Which word in paragraph D. means "take without permission"?_____

6. Which word in paragraph D. means "have a proper place"?_____

7. Which word in paragraph E. means "found guilty"?_____

8. Which word in paragraph E. means "perplexed"?_____

9. Which word in paragraph G. means "institution for children without parents"?_____

10. Which word in paragraph H. means "pity"?_____

C. Return to Exercise A. Place two check marks (✔✔) in front of the word in COLUMN II that is the ANTONYM of the word in COLUMN I. Read aloud a complete sentence using this word.

D. Select one of the three (3) words (phrases) that best fulfills the MEANING of the sentence according to the narrative. Insert the word in the blank space. Read the completed sentence aloud.

1. Curtis Smith was in trouble because he wanted to be a_____.
   a. misanthrope   b. philanthropist   c. teacher

2. Mrs. Smith called on Mr. Campbell because she_____.
   a. needed counsel   b. needed money   c. liked Mike

3. The busing was ordered to offer children equal_____.
   a. education   b. law   c. income

4. Mr. Campbell was a good _____ and he _____ attentively.
   a. man, looked   b. friend, talked   c. lawyer, listened

5. Curtis was_____ one call because it was his_____.
   a. given,   b. allowed,   c. ordered, mother
      custody cal   constitutional right   talking

6. To convict a man the court must know beyond a reasonable_____ that a man is_____.
   a. doubt, guilty   b. thought, covered up   c. doubt, innocent

7. The judge _____ an _____ of Curtis' personal activities.
   a. dispersed, court b. ordered,   c. covered up,
                           investigation   examination

8. The court_____ to_____ time for the examination.
   a. reconvened,   b. met again,   c. recessed,
      convict   disperse   allow

9. Curtis' peers avoided him at first because he was_____.
   a. not well-to-do   b. a tackle   c. a bad boy

10. The money was donated to the orphanage to _____ the war orphans.
    a. consider   b. discard   c. sustain

11. The judge was_____ because Curtis stole to_____ to the orphanage
    a. lenient,   b. severe, give   c. deliberate, travel
       contribute

IX. Comprehension [Exercises]

A. Place a check mark (✔) in front of the correct response to each of the statements according to the narrative. Read the complete sentence aloud.

1. At the age of sixteen, Curtis was
   _____ a. the oldest of the children.
   _____ b. the second oldest of the children.
   _____ c. the best of the children.

2. The house where Curtis lived
_____ a. was overcrowded.
_____ b. was wrong.
_____ c. was old.

3. Mrs. Smith came to Mr. Campbell because
_____ a. she needed money.
_____ b. she knew Mike.
_____ c. she needed counsel.

4. Mr. Campbell helped Mrs. Smith because
_____ a. she was a good housekeeper.
_____ b. she was his friend.
_____ c. Curtis was in deep trouble.

5. Curtis was Mike's friend. They were on the
_____ a. football team together.
_____ b. wrong side of the tracks.
_____ c. orphanage.

6. The busing was intended for
_____ a. the Campbell family.
_____ b. the children of lower income households.
_____ c. the law.

7. Mr. Campbell took notes to use them
_____ a. in court.
_____ b. a t home.
_____ c. for Mike.

8. Mr. Campbell assured Mrs. Smith
_____ a. that Curtis was innocent.
_____ b. that he would do all he could.
_____ c. that the police were kind.

9. The one phone call at the police station

_____ a. is a constitutional right.

_____ b. is a police kindness.

_____ c. is not a right of everyone.

10. The people whispered in the courtroom

_____ a. because they were kind.

_____ b. because they were unkind.

_____ c. because they liked Curtis.

11. The judge rapped his gavel

_____ a. for the recess.

_____ b. to restore silence.

_____ c. to maintain Curtis' innocence.

12. The judge ordered an investigation

_____ a. of Curtis' friends.

_____ b. of Curtis' personal activities.

_____ c. of the guards.

13. Curtis gave the money

_____ a. to his friends.

_____ b. to the football team.

_____ c. to the orphanage.

14. When Curtis contributed, he became

_____ a. a victim

_____ b. a tackle.

_____ c. one of the team.

15. The judge was kind because he

_____ a. gave a suspended sentence.

_____ b. rapped his gavel.

_____ c. deliberated quietly.

B. Below there are three (3) different thoughts expressed in each of the exercises. Assign the proper sequence (order) of THOUGHT, according to the narrative, by numbering 1 to 3. Read aloud.

1. a. he was the second oldest
    b. at the age of sixteen
    c. child in the family

2. a. where he lived
    b. was overcrowded but clean
    c. the house

3. a. called on Mr. Campbell
    b. to seek counsel
    c. Mrs. Smith

4. a. of lower income households
    b. the authorities intended to offer
    c. equal educational opportunity to children

5. a. to use in court
    b. he made many notes
    c. which he was going

6. a. to do all he could for Curtis
    b. that he was going
    c. he assured Mrs. Smith

7. a. constitutional right
    b. was his
    c. the one phone call

8. a. fingers at Curtis
    b. the warehouse guards
    c. pointed accusing

9. a. they testified
    b. broke into the warehouse
    c. he was the man who

10. a. and then they steal from us
    b. over our schools
    c. first they take

11. a. they belong
    b. stay where
    c. they should

12. a. his innocence
    b. Curtis' friends and
    c. neighbors maintained

13. a. who never did wrong
    b. that he was a good boy
    c. they declared under oath

14. a. doubt that a man is guilty
    b. must know beyond reasonable
    c. the court

15. a. activities was ordered
    b. of Curtis' personal
    c. a thorough investigation

16. a. by the investigation
    b. the following was revealed
    c. when the court reconvened

17. a. they did not treat him as an equal
    b. even when he was accepted
    c. as a tackle on the team

18. a. an orphanage in a small town
    b. the team adopted
    c. when the war broke out overseas

19. a. to sustain the war victims
    b. was sent there which helped
    c. each month a contribution

20. a. for the stolen goods
    b. went to the orphanage
    c. the money which he received

21. a. quietly with
    b. the prosecuting attorney
    c. the judge deliberated

22. a. we cannot take stern
    b. in view of the circumstances
    c. measures against the accused

23. a. in the custody
    b. of his parents
    c. we place Curtis Smith

C. There are some statements listed below about the narrative.
    Write **T** in front of each statement that you think is true.
    Write **F** if the statement is not true. Read aloud.

    _____ 1.   Curtis Smith came from a low income family.

    _____ 2.   He was the second oldest in his family.

    _____ 3.   The house where Curtis lived was spacious.

    _____ 4.   The Smith family was well-to-do.

_____ 5. Curtis was in no trouble.

_____ 6. Curtis was Mike Campbell's friend.

_____ 7. The busing was ordered by the authorities.

_____ 8. Mike and Curtis were on the football team.

_____ 9. Mr. Campbell did not listen to Mrs. Smith.

_____ 10. He promised to do all he could for Curtis.

_____ 11. The judge was perplexed.

_____ 12. He ordered a complete examination.

_____ 13. Those present in the courtroom whispered.

_____ 14. Curtis' neighbors pointed accusing fingers.

_____ 15. He could be convicted on reasonable doubt.

_____ 16. When Curtis came to Euclid High his peers liked him.

_____ 17. They treated him like an equal.

_____ 18. Curtis did not want to contribute to the orphanage.

_____ 19. He took money from the war victims.

_____ 20. The judge deliberated noisily with the prosecuting attorney.

_____ 21. The court took stern measures with Curtis.

X. Composition and Discussion

A. In COLUMN I are the beginnings of sentences. In COLUMN II are the completions to sentences of COLUMN I. Select the completion best fitting each sentence in COLUMN I according to the narrative. Read the completed sentences orally. Compose new sentences orally and discuss the narrative.

COLUMN I   COLUMN II

1. Curtis Smith came   a. in the custody of his parents.

2. At the age of sixteen   b. lenient with Curtis.

3. The hope where Curtis lived   c. he was the second oldest.

4. Mrs. Smith called on   d. by the authorities.
    Mr. Campbell

5. Curtis Smith attended   e. to seek counsel.

6. The busing was ordered   f. on the same football team.

7. Mike and Curtis were   g. for one week.

8. Mr. Campbell made   h. a thorough investigation.

9. He was going to do all   i. contribute money to war victims.

10. The phone call was   j. Mike Campbell's high school.

11. The warehouse guards   k. broke into the warehouse.

12. They testified that he   l. was overcrowded but clean.

13. Curtis' friends and neighbors   m. pointed accusing fingers at Curtis.

14. The judge ordered   n. many notes.

15. The court recessed   o. from a Negro family.

16. Curtis stole to   p. maintained that he was a good boy.

17. The court was   q. Curtis' constitutional right.

18. Curtis was placed   r. he could for Curtis.

B. 1. Tell us what you know about a philanthropist.

2. Describe circumstances in lower income households.

3. Tell us what you think of Curtis Smith's action.

4. Tell us what you think of Curtis' friends and neighbors.

5. Tell us what you think of Curtis' friends at Euclid High.

C. Describe what you see in the picture below.

D. Read the poem aloud. Answer orally the questions listed following the poem

The Boy with the Golden Hair

The sweet smile that brightens [1] *the dark of day,*	[1] makes happy
the cry of joy when loved ones are at hand [2]	[2] present
contentment [3] *shining from the loving eyes.*	[3] pleasure
all these are part of the Boy with the golden hair...	
He falls, the guilt [4] *and pain are mine,*	[4] offense
for I was slow although my eyes perceived. [5]	[5] saw
Don't cry, my little star, my sweet little	
Boy with the golden hair...	
The grateful [6] *touch of soft and precious* [7] *hands,*	[6] thankful
the kiss of tiny lips upon a coarse [8] *and many cheek.*	[7] wonderful
All these are mine-my image [9] *he-and I the father of*	[8] rough
they Boy with the golden hair...	[9] picture
And when at close of day a frown [10] *is forced upon my brow*	[10] sullen
because of the labors past and dreams still unfulfilled, [11]	[11] not done
but for the touch. This smile... This tear... All gone...	
but he, the Boy with the golden hair...	

    1. Identify the indefinite pronouns in this poem.
    2. Identify all adjectives describing the boy.
    3. Identify the person speaking in the third verse.
    4. What is the main idea here?

CHAPTER FOUR

THE

RELUCTANT WARD

IN THIS CHAPTER

Words to remember:
Obligation with *should, ought, had better, have to*

Prepositions:
in, on, at, to

Possessive Determiners:
my, your, his, her, its, our, your, their

I. Narrative

A. Lori came to the *adoptive* agency under emotional and physical neglect. Because of the *cruelty* of her parents she was in the custody of the agency. The agency made it *known* in a newspaper *article* that Lori was *available* for adoption. Mrs. Campbell answered the article. She called the *welfare* agency and asked to see Lori.

B. The first time she saw Lori, Mrs. Campbell knew she *had better* speak to the agent about her. The child was eight years old. Signs of *abuse* were *evident*. There was a large *bruise* under the girl's left eye. Lori's manners were different. She seemed more mature than most children eight years of age. Her large eyes had a look of *sadness* in them. Mrs. Campbell learned from the social worker that Lori had been unable to stay in two foster homes previously. They only increased her emotional problems.

---

adoptive: taking a child into a family
cruelty: brutality
known: public
article: report
available: accessible
welfare: social service
had better: ought to
abuse: hurt
evident: easy to see
bruise: injury
sadness: depression
needed: desired
distrust: doubt, suspicion
ran away: escaped
found: discovered
wandering about: walking around

treated: handled
quietly: softly
understanding: sympathy
pack: put things together
belongings: property
sincerity: honesty
request: petition
disturb: interfere (with)
visitors: guests
approached: came closer
black eye: bruised eye
attack: use force
replied: answered
silent: quiet
closer: nearer
feeling: sensation

C.   Even though Lori was mistreated at home, she always returned there. Lori said that her little sister and her infant brother *needed* her. "The capacity to feel in Lori is extraordinary," said the social worker. "And she doesn't know about her illness, though it's terminal. This is also the reason for her lack of physical development." Mrs. Campbell said, "We'll do all we can for her when she comes to us."

D.   Somehow, Lori remained withdrawn, full of tension and *distrust* toward the Campbell family. She refused food at first. Mrs. Campbell feared for Lori's health. The girl locked herself in her room for hours at a time. She *ran away* once. They *found* her *wandering about* in the neighborhood.

E.   But love had a way of overcoming anxiety and distrust. The Campbell children were especially helpful. They *treated* their new sister with the same rough affection with which they treated one another. She was to feel useful and needed. Gradually, she opened her heart to her new family.

F.   Several months went by. One Sunday morning, Lori put her arms around her "mother's" neck affectionately. "I have to go home now," she said *quietly*. Mrs. Campbell looked at Lori with *under-standing*. "Okay," she said. "Let's *pack* your things. We'll go after breakfast. But we must first get your things ready."

G.   Mrs. Campbell helped Lori with her *belongings*. The *sincerity* of Lori's *request* did not *disturb* her. However, it was a difficult test for both of them, she knew. As they were leaving the house, Mrs. Campbell got the car keys off the hall table. Soon, they arrived at the old place where Lori used to live. Mrs. Campbell felt her pulse quicken.

H.   The woman sat on the dirty sofa reading a newspaper. Lori ran toward the little girl who sat on the floor. "Linda! Linda!" Lori exclaimed excitedly. It was then the woman turned toward the *visitors*. The little girl *approached* her sister clumsily. She had a *black eye*. Lori kissed the little one affectionately. The woman became hysterical. She was about to *attack* Lori when Mrs. Campbell quickly interfered.

I.   It was not until she was safe in the car that Lori spoke. "I love you Mother Campbell." "I love you too, dear," Mrs. Campbell *replied*. "You know, Mother, I know we have to help them, but I guess there's no way we can do it." Lori didn't cry and she didn't complain. She was *silent*. "Who knows, darling, maybe you can help them after all," Mrs. Campbell said with a mysterious twinkle in her eyes. Lori moved *closer* to her mother. It was a good *feeling*.

Idea Questions:

1. Why did Lori come to the adoptive agency?

2. What was different about Lori? Describe her.

3. Why did Lori always return to her old home?

4. Do you know why Lori distrusted the Campbells?

5. How did the Campbells overcome Lori's distrust?

6. Was it a good idea to take Lori to her old home?

7. What kind of a woman was Lori's mother?

8. How was Lori's mother different from Mrs. Campbell?

9. Why did Lori say "I love you" to Mrs. Campbell?

10. What is the MAIN IDEA of this story?

II. Words in Context [Pictographs]

Below are the words used in the narrative. Where possible, each word has a [synonym]; or it is defined as used in the story. Where possible, an antonym is also given. Make up sentences about the pictographs choosing the words you need. Read aloud.

Example: *(calm)*= Lori was not calm

Drawing of paragraphs A, B & C

A. B. and C.

agency [**department**]; abuse [**maltreatment**] *(care)*; bruise [**black and blue spot**]; cruel [**brutal**] *(gentle)*; emotional [**mental**] *(physical)*; evident [**clear**] *(concealed)*; neglect [**disregard**] *(care)*; physical [**bodily**] *(mental)*; reluctant [**hesitant**] *(willing)*; ward [**adopted person**]; welfare [**social service**]; manners [**habitual or customary behavior**]; seem [**appear**] *(conceal)*; mature [**grown up**] *(immature)*; sad [**depressed**] *(happy)*; learn [**be informed by**] *(ignore)*; social [**public**] *(personal)*; foster [**adopted**]; previous [**prior**] *(subsequent)*; increase [**grow**] *(diminish)*; problem [**difficulty**] *(solution)*; mistreat [**injure**] *(care for)*; return [**come back**] *(leave)*; infant [**child**] *(adult)*; capacity [**skill**] *(inability)*; feel [**be concerned**] *(ignore)*; extraordinary [**remarkable**] *(common)*; illness [**sickness**] *(health)*; terminal [**incurable**] *(curable)*; lack [**want**] *(supply)*; develop [**grow**] *(deteriorate)*; face it [**cope**] *(avoid)*

Drawing of paragraphs D & E

D. and E.

remain [**continue**] *(discontinue)*; withdraw [**retreat**] *(emerge)*; tension [**anxiety**] *(relaxation)*; refuse [**decline**] *(accept)*; fear [**dread**] *(trust)*; agency [**department**]; abuse [**maltreatment**] *(care)*; bruise [**black and blue spot**]; cruel [**brutal**] *(gentle)*; emotional [**mental**] *(calm)*; evident [**clear**] *(concealed)*; neglect [**disregard**] *(care)*; physical [**bodily**] *(mental)*; rough [**boisterous**] *(gentle)*; useful [**helpful**] *(useless)*; gradual [**step by step**] *(sudden)*; open [**show her feelings**] *(become more withdrawn)*; heart [**center of emotions**]; run away [**go away**] *(stay)*; wander [**stroll about aimlessly**] *(walk purposefully)*

Drawing of paragraphs F, G, H & I

F. G. H. and I.

Affectionate [**tender**] *(indifferent)*; neck [**the part of man joining the head and body**]; reply [**answer**] *(ignore)*; sincere [**honest**] *(feigned)*; difficult [**hard**] *(easy)*; leave [**depart**] *(return)*; hall [**corridor**]; pulse [**heartbeat**]; quicken [**accelerate**] *(slow down)*; dirty [**filthy**] *(clean)*; sofa [**couch**]; excited [**enthusiastic**] *(passive)*; clumsy [**awkward**] *(graceful)*; speechless [**without words**] *(talkative)*; hysterical [**uncontrolled**] *(calm)*; quick [**prompt**] *(slow)*; interfere [**come between**] *(not become involved)*; attack [**assault**] *(defend)*; until [**before**] *(afterward)*; guess [**suppose**] *(be certain)*; cry [**weep**] (laugh); complain [**whine**] *(approve)*; maybe [**perhaps**] *(impossible)*; mysterious [**secret**] *(obvious)*; twinkle [**sparkle**] *(be expressionless)*; move [**transfer**] *(remain)*

III. Structure [Phrases]

Below are some phrases taken from the narrative. Make complete sentences and read them aloud.

1. **to**	- come	- the		- adoptive agency
2. **because**		- of the		- cruelty
3. **be**	-Lori	- in		- custody
4. **up**	- she	- for	- be	- adoption
5. **the**		- first		- time
6. **be**		- eight years		- old
7. **signs**		- of		- abuse
8. **a**		- look		- of sadness
9. **for**		- hours		- at a time
10. **like**		- to go		- home
11. **closer**		- to	- move	- her mother

IV. Sentences

A. Read the following sentences aloud. Repeat, substituting where possible, a synonym of the word in italics, or a phrase that explains the meaning. Make other necessary changes.

> Example: She was an *extraordinary* woman
> She was a *remarkable* woman

1. Because of her parents' *cruelty*, Lori was in custody.
2. The agency made it *known* in a newspaper article.
3. The child was *agitated*.
4. Signs of abuse were *evident*.
5. She was *reluctant* to stay in foster homes.
6. Lori always *returned* home.
7. Her *capacity* to feel was extraordinary.
8. She doesn't know about her *illness*.

9. Mrs. Campbell knew Lori's illness was *terminal.*

10. The Campbell children *remained* helpful.

11. Lori *withdrew* from everyone.

12. She *refused* to accept them.

13. Lori *feared* her real home.

14. Mrs. Campbell *helped* Lori to overcome fear.

15. Lori approached her little sister with *love.*

16. Mrs. Campbell *displayed* distrust toward the woman.

17. The woman wanted to *attack* her daughter.

18. Mrs. Campbell's reaction was *quick.*

B. Fill in the blanks with words from the narrative. Each space may be filled by a word or phrase. Do not refer back to the narrative. Where possible, use variations of the missing words. Read aloud.

Lori _____ came the adoptive _____. She was _____ custody_____ the agency. They made it _____ a newspaper article that Lori was _____ adoption. Mrs. Campbell knew she _____ speak _____ the agent.

Signs _____ abuse were _____. Lori's _____ were different. She _____ more mature _____ most children eight years _____ age. Her eyes had a _____ sadness _____ them. Lori had been _____ stay _____ two foster homes.

Even though Lori was _____ home, she always _____ there. "The capacity _____ feel _____ Lori is _____," said the _____ worker. Mrs. Campbell said, "We'll do _____ we can _____ her when she _____ us."

Lori refused _____ first. Mrs. Campbell feared _____ Lori's _____. The girl _____ herself _____ her room for a _____ time. She _____ once. She was wandering _____ the _____.

Love has a _____ overcoming _____ and _____. The children were _____ helpful. Lori was made _____ feel _____ and _____.

Several _____ went _____. One _____ morning, Lori put _____ arms round _____ "mother's" neck. " I_____ go home now," she _____. Mrs. Campbell looked _____ Lori with _____.

Mrs. Campbell _____ Lori with _____ belongings. The _____ of Lori's _____ did not _____ her. It was a _____ test for both _____ them. They _____ at the old _____ where Lori used to _____. Mrs. Campbell _____ her pulse _____.

The woman sat _____ the _____ sofa. Lori _____ toward the _____ girl. "Linda! Linda!" Lori exclaimed _____. The woman turned _____ the visitors. The little_____ had a _____ eye. Lori _____ her sister _____. The woman became _____.

It was not _____ she was _____ in the car _____ Lori spoke. "I _____ you Mother Campbell." Lori didn't _____ and she didn't _____. She was _____. She moved closer _____ mother. It was a _____.

V. Grammar (Points of Interest)

A. 1. When positive **obligation** or **advisability** is expressed we use the words *should* or *ought*

Mike *should* (or *ought* to) help his friends

The helping verb we use here is *had better*

When she saw Lori, Mrs. Campbell knew she *had better* speak to the agent.

2. *Have to + verb* means that *it is necessary* to do something.

"I *have to* go home now," Lori said.
"I know we *have* to help them," she said.

B. Prepositions *in, on, at,* and *to (toward)* answer the question *where (to)?*

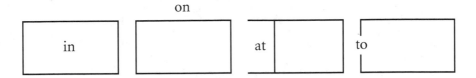

She was *in* custody of the agency.
They made it known *in* a newspaper article.

The little girl sat *on* the floor.
The woman sat *on* the sofa.

They arrived *at* the old place.
Lori was mistreated *at* home.

Lori came *to* the adoptive agency.
We'll do all we can for when she comes *to* us.

She was full of tension and distrust *toward* the Campbell family.

[Other uses of prepositions are discussed elsewhere.]

C. The *possessive determiner* [case] forms are:

I	- *my*	I have to help *my* little sister.
you	-*your*	*Your* child has a terminal illness.
he	- *his*	*His* mother came to visit.
she	- *her*	*Her* brother was abused.
it	- *its*	The child went on *its* way.
we	- *our*	We will treat her like *our* own.
you	- *your*	They say *your* mother is nice.
they	- *their*	They treated *their* new sister well.

VI. Word Recognition

A. Circle the word (phrase) in Column II that is most like the word in Column I, and the word (phrase) in Column III most unlike the word in Column I. This oral identification of words ought to be timed.

COLUMN I	COLUMN II	COLUMN III
1. **abuse**	a. operation b. maltreatment c. agency	a. break b. interference c. care
2. **attack**	a. be quick b. be prompt c. assault	a. defend b. interfere c. come between
3. **clumsy**	a. speechless b. awkward c. without words	a. talkative b. calm c. graceful
4. **complain**	a. whine b. care c. approve	a. return b. rejoice c. want
5. **cruel**	a. brutal b. bruised c. broken	a. respected b. gentle c. healing
6. **difficult**	a. bad b. good c. hard	a. open b. simple c. tough
7. **dirty**	a. filthy b. bad c. rough	a. open b. free c. clean

8. **distrust**
   a. anxiety
   b. eagerness
   c. suspicion

   a. contentment
   b. trust
   c. hatred

9. **evident**
   a. gentle
   c. clear
   b. brutal

   a. reluctant
   b. concealed
   c. unwilling

10. **gradual**
   a. affectionate
   b. slow
   c. tender

   a. sudden
   b. indifferent
   c. dishonest

11. **guess**
   a. cry
   b. suppose
   c. weep

   a. prove
   b. laugh
   c. complain

12. **infant**
   a. child
   b. doctor
   c. boy

   a. adult
   b. doctor
   c. person

B. Pick the right expression. Complete the following sentences with the term that best fits the situation. Read aloud.

lock	mistreat	open
develop	quick	extraordinary
previous	increase	incurable
mature	remain	capacity
refuse	neglect	rough
sad	terminal	physical

1. If an illness is incurable, we call it _____.

2. A grown up person is expected to be _____.

3. If you injure another person, you _____ him.

4. When we say that something is remarkable,
    we call it _____.

5. If someone comes under physical disregard, we can also say that he is under physical _____.

6. When problems grow, we can also say they _____.

7. When we reject something, we _____ it.

8. If we wished to stay somewhere, we would _____ there.

9. Bodily injury is _____.

10. A depressed person is also _____.

C. In the space on the left write the word(s) that would best fit the expression in **bold print**. Make other necessary changes. Read aloud.

_____ 1. Lori came to the **adoptive** agency.

_____ 2. Signs of **improper treatment** were evident.

_____ 3. Her parents were **cruel**.

_____ 4. Lori was under **physical** neglect.

_____ 5. She was **reluctant** to stay in foster homes.

_____ 6. Lori's **manners** were different.

_____ 7. She seemed more **mature** than other children.

_____ 8. She looked **depressed**.

_____ 9. **Prior** to that she had stayed in two foster homes.

_____ 10. They increased her emotional **difficulties**.

_____ 11. The children were **injured**.

_____ 12. She always **came back** to her home.

_____ 13. Her **skill** to feel is extraordinary.

_____ 14. Her **sickness** is terminal.

_____ 15. This is the reason for the lack of **well-being**.

_____ 16. Lori **stayed** withdrawn.

_____ 17. **Love** overcomes anxiety.

_____ 18. The Campbell children were **particularly** helpful.

_____ 19. **Slowly**, she opened her heart.

_____ 20. Once she **strolled** through the neighborhood.

_____ 21. Lori was **tender** with Mrs. Campbell.

_____ 22. She **answered** quietly.

_____ 23. It was **hard** to understand.

_____ 24. She wanted to **depart** from home.

_____ 25. The woman became **uncontrolled.**

VII. Concept Recognition

Fill in the most appropriate word (phrase) to express the CONCEPT of the sentence according to the narrative. Read the complete sentences aloud.

A. Because Lori was under _____ and _____ neglect, she came to the adoptive agency.
   1. emotional, physical   3. calm, unwilling
   2. uncertain, immaterial   4. reluctant, material

B. Lori was in custody because of the _____ of her parents.
   1. gentleness   3. welfare
   2. cruelty   4. ill luck

C. Lori was not like other girls, she had different _____.
   1. design   3. manners
   2. neglect   4. problems

D. Lori left other foster homes because they _____ her emotional problems.
   1. diminished   3. returned
   2. appeared   4. increased

E. She returned home to _____ her little sister and brother.
  1. help   3. feel
  2. develop   4. increase

F. Her physical development was retarded because of the _____ illness.
  1. temporary   3. terminal
  2. prior   4. mature

G. Lori was mistreated, but her capacity to _____ was extraordinary.
  1. supply   3. develop
  2. feel   4. expand

H. Mrs. Campbell feared for Lori's health because the girl was _____ and _____ food.
  1. withdrawn, refused   3. offered, accepted
  2. strained, relaxed   4. expanded, dwarfed

I. When Lori ran away, they found her _____ about in the neighborhood.
  1. wandering   3. overcome
  2. succumbed   4. locked

J. The Campbell children were roughly affectionate to Lori, and this was _____.
  1. worthless   3. helpful
  2. gradual   4. slow

K. In order to go home Lori had to _____ her things.
  1. leave   3. pack
  2. accelerate   4. return

L. Mrs. Campbell helped Lori because she _____ the girl.
  1. ignored   3. loved
  2. answered   4. replied

M. Lori was _____ when she saw her little sister.
1. excited
2. uncontrolled
3. hysterical
4. calm

N. Mrs. Campbell and Lori left the old house because the woman was about to _____ Lori.
1. love
2. move
3. attack
4. calm

VIII. Telling the Meaning

A. Place a check mark in front of the word in Column II that best fits the MEANING of the word in Column I. Read aloud a complete sentence using this word.

COLUMN I   COLUMN II

1. **accelerate**   _____ a. quicken
                         _____ b. slow down
                         _____ c. pulsate

2. **affectionate**   _____ a. tender
                         _____ b. indifferent
                         _____ c. difficult

3. **boisterous**   _____ a. gentle
                         _____ b. rough
                         _____ c. overcome

4. **brutal**   _____ a. cruel
                         _____ b. gentle
                         _____ c. emotional

5. **clear**   _____ a. uncertain
                         _____ b. evident
                         _____ c. calm

6. **confine**

_____ a. open
_____ b. lock
_____ c. love

7. **develop**

_____ a. grow
_____ b. dwarf
_____ c. avoid

8. **excited**

_____ a. aroused
_____ b. passive
_____ c. clumsy

9. **extraordinary**

_____ a. common
_____ b. examined
_____ c. remarkable

10. **fear**

_____ a. trust
_____ b. dread
_____ c. refuse

11. **filthy**

_____ a. excited
_____ b. dirty
_____ c. clean

12. **hysterical**

_____ a. uncontrolled
_____ b. calm
_____ c. sweet

13. **increase**

_____ a. diminish
_____ b. grow
_____ c. doubt

14. **interference**

_____ a. not become involved
_____ b. come between
_____ c. safety

15. **lack**

_____ a. want
_____ b. supply
_____ c. develop

B. Recognize words in the Narrative

1. Which word in paragraph **A.** means "maltreatment"? _____

2. Which word in paragraph **A.** means "taking a child into a family"? _____

3. Which word in paragraph **B.** means "black and blue spot"?

    _____

4. Which word in paragraph **B.** means "habitual behavior"?

    _____

5. Which word in paragraph **B.** means "grown up"? _____

6. Which word in paragraph **C.** means "incurable"? _____

7. Which word in paragraph **D.** means "well-being"? _____

8. Which word in paragraph **E.** means "step by step"? _____

9. Which word in paragraph **F.** means "tender"? _____

10. Which word in paragraph **G.** means "honest"? _____

11. Which word in paragraph **G.** means "accelerate"? _____

12. Which word in paragraph **H.** means "enthusiastic"? _____

13. Which word in paragraph **H.** means "awkward"? _____

14. Which word in paragraph **I.** means "suppose"? _____

15. Which word in paragraph **I.** means "secret"? _____

C. Return to Exercise A. Place two check marks in front of the word in COLUMN II that is the ANTONYM of the word in COLUMN I. Read aloud a complete sentence using this word.

D. Select one of the three (3) words (phrases) that best fulfills the MEANING of the sentence according to the narrative. Insert the word in the blank space. Read the completed sentence aloud.

1. Lori was at the adoptive agency because she was _____ at home.
   a. mistreated   b. calm   c. uncontrolled

2. Mrs. Campbell wanted to adopt Lori so that she could _____ her.
   a. respect   b. help   c. neglect

3. Lori's manners were different because she seemed more _____.
   a. mature   b. gentle   c. material

4. Mrs. Campbell learned about Lori's _____ from the social worker.
   a. mature feeling   b. emotional problems   c. sister

5. Lori always returned home to _____ her sister and brother.
   a. help   b. supply   c. ignore

6. Because of her experience, Lori had an _____ to feel.
   a. sad certainty   b. doubt problem   c. extraordinary capacity

7. Lori distrusted the Campbells and remained _____.
   a. withdrawn   b. relaxed   c. happy

8. The Campbells loved her and Lori _____ her _____ and distrust.
   a. ignored, fear   b. overcame, anxiety   c. doubt, problem

9. When Lori wanted to go home, Mrs. Campbell _____ she would lose her.
   a. appeared   b. wanted   c. feared

10. When the woman became _____ , Lori knew her home was with the Campbells.
    a. hysterical   b. extraordinary   c. affectionate

IX. Comprehension [Exercises]

A. Place a check mark in front of the correct response to each of the following statements according to the narrative. Read the complete-sentence aloud.

1. Lori was in custody of the agency because
    _____a. she was a child of eleven.
    _____b. of the cruelty of her parents.
    _____c. she liked her sister.

2. A newspaper article made it known that
    _____a. Lori was up for adoption.
    _____b. Lori was ill.
    _____c. Lori was at the Campbell's.

3. Mrs. Campbell learned about Lori from
    _____a. her neighbors.
    _____b. the agency.
    _____c. the newspaper.

4. Lori's manners were different because
    _____a. she was a girl.
    _____b. she seemed more mature.
    _____c. she was depressed.

5. Lori always returned to her home
    _____a. to see her mother.
    _____b. to run away.
    _____c. to help her little sister and brother.

6. Lori lacked physical development because
    _____a. of her illness.
    _____b. of her inability to feel.
    _____c. of her want.

7. The Campbells were kind to Lori because
_____a. they loved her.
_____b. they needed her.
_____c. they played with her.

8. The Campbell children helped Lori
_____a. with her housework.
_____b. overcome her anxiety and distrust.
_____c. with her family.

9. When Mrs. Campbell took Lori home, she
_____a. cried.
_____b. packed her things.
_____c. was afraid.

10. Mrs. Campbell knew it was going to be
_____a. a difficult test for both of them.
_____b. a nice ride to town.
_____c. a remarkable experience.

11. When Lori saw Linda she was
_____a. very depressed.
_____b. very excited.
_____c. very ill.

12. When the woman saw Lori
_____a. she got very depressed.
_____b. she got hysterical.
_____c. she was happy.

13. On the way back to the Campbell's
_____a. Lori didn't cry.
_____b. Lori cried.
_____c. Lori was very neglected.

14. Lori wished she could
_____a. stay with her mother.
_____b. stay with the Campbells.
_____c. help her brother and sister.

15. When Lori moved closer to Mrs. Campbell,
    _____a. it was rough.
    _____b. it was a good feeling.
    _____c. it was a twinkle.

B. Below there are three (3) different thoughts expressed in each of the exercises. Assign the proper sequence (order) of THOUGHT, according to the narrative, by numbering 1 to 3. Read aloud.

1. a. in a newspaper article _____
   b. the agency made it known _____
   c. that Lori was up for adoption _____

2. a. in the custody of the agency _____
   b. of her parents, she was _____
   c. because of the cruelty _____

3. a. and asked to see Lori _____
   b. the welfare agency _____
   c. she called _____

4. a. speak to the agent about her _____
   b. the first time she saw Lori _____
   c. Mrs. Campbell knew she had better _____

5. a. eight years of age _____
   b. mature than most children _____
   c. she seemed more _____

6. a. sadness in them _____
   b. had a look of _____
   c. her large eyes _____

7. a. she always returned there _____
   b. was mistreated at home _____
   c. even though Lori _____

8. a. when she comes to us
    b. we can for her
    c. we'll do all

9. a. for hours at a time
    b. in her room
    c. the girl locked herself

10. a. they treated one another
    b. the same rough affection with which
    c. they treated their new sister with

11. a. ready after breakfast
    b. as you have your things
    c. we'll go as soon

12. a. as they were leaving the house,
    b. the car keys off the hall table
    c. Mrs. Campbell got

13. a. where Lori used to live
    b. soon they arrived
    c. at the old place

14. a. reading a newspaper
    b. the woman sat
    c. on the dirty sofa

15. a. that Lori spoke
    b. it was not until
    c. she was safe in the car

16. a. help them after all
    b. who knows, my child,
    c. maybe you can

C. There are some statements listed below about the narrative.
Write **T** for **True** in front of each statement that you think is true.
Write **F** for **False** if the statement is not true. Read aloud.

_____ 1. Lori came to the adoptive agency, calmly.

_____ 2. She was in custody because of the cruelty of her parents.

_____ 3. Mrs. Campbell learned about Lori from a newspaper article.

_____ 4. When Mrs. Campbell saw Lori there was a large bruise under her eye.

_____ 5. Lori's manners were like most children her age.

_____ 6. Lori seemed more mature than most children her age.

_____ 7. Her large eyes had a happy look.

_____ 8. Lori stayed in four foster homes.

_____ 9. Lori returned to her home because she was treated well.

_____ 10. Lori had a common capacity to feel.

_____ 11. Lori had a temporary illness.

_____ 12. At first, Lori remained withdrawn.

_____ 13. She ate well at first.

_____ 14. Mrs. Campbell had trust in Lori's health.

_____ 15. Lori ran away once.

_____ 16. The Campbell children treated Lori like one of them.

_____ 17. They made her feel useless.

_____ 18. One Sunday morning Lori asked to be taken home.

_____ 19. Mrs. Campbell told Lori not to go.

_____ 20. The woman reading the paper was Lori's mother.

_____ 21. The woman was calm when she saw Lori.

_____ 22. When they left, Lori cried and complained.

_____ 23. Mrs. Campbell was affectionate with Lori.

X. Composition and Discussion

A. In COLUMN I are the beginnings of sentences. In COLUMN II are the completions to sentences of COLUMN I. Select the completion best fitting each sentence in COLUMN I according to the narrative. Read the completed sentences orally. Compose new sentences orally and discuss the narrative.

COLUMN I	COLUMN II
1. Lori came to the adoptive agency	a. she always returned there.
2. Because of the cruelty of her parents	b. than most children eight years of age.
3. Mrs. Campbell called	c. for her when she comes to us.
4. The child was	d. under emotional and physical neglect.
5. Signs of abuse	e. in Lori was extraordinary.
6. She seemed more mature	f. of overcoming anxiety and distrust.
7. Her large eyes had	g. were especially helpful.
8. Even though Lori was mistreated at home	h. her heart to her new family.
9. The capacity to feel	i. were evident.
10. We'll do all we can	j. for Lori's health.
11. She refused food	k. she was in the custody of the agency.
12. Mrs. Campbell feared	l. at first.
13. They found her wandering	m. little girl who sat on the floor.
14. But love had a way	n. with her belongings.
15. The Campbell children	o. reading a newspaper.
16. Gradually, she opened	p. a look of sadness in them.
17. Mrs. Campbell helped Lori	q. about in the neighborhood.
18. The woman sat on the dirty sofa	r. the welfare agency.
19. Lori ran toward the	s. eight years old.

B. 1. Tell us what you know about Lori.

2. Tell us about Lori's family.

3. What do you know about a welfare agency?

4. How did the Campbell family accept Lori?

5. Describe Lori's visit to her old home.

C. Describe what you see in the picture below.

D. Read the poem aloud. Answer orally the questions listed following the poem.

     Hospitality[1]   [1]cordiality

The soul,[2] and then into   [2]spirit
the smallest recesses[3]   [3]niche
of my heart came
the ineffable[4] feeling   [4]inexpressible
of happiness.

Can it cease[5] to exist   [5]stop
because of mere
mortality?[6] Then   [6]death

should we be destined[7]   [7]fated
to meet there
at the crossroads of
our life-span,[8]   [8]lifetime

if I were first,
or you, or both
we were together,

do again, as you
have done before!
The memory[9] of joy[10]   [9]recollection
will stay... mine...   [10]happiness
perhaps forevermore..?

1. Identify all *possessive determiners*.
2. Identify all *prepositions*.
3. Which verse expresses happiness? Why?
4. What wish is expressed in the last verse?

CHAPTER FIVE

THE WOULD

BE PRESIDENT

IN THIS CHAPTER

Words to remember:
have + past participle

Future Time:
will, I'll or Shall + infinitive

request-question

Possessive pronouns:
mine, yours, his, hers, its, ours, yours, theirs

place:	*where?*
manner:	*how?*
time:	*when?*

I. Narrative

A. Mike had never been this excited before. He came home from school earlier than usual. "Mom!" he *yelled*. "I'm *running for* president of our student council!" Mrs. Campbell sensed something unusual in her son's behavior. "Let's have a cola, Mike" she suggested, "and you can tell me all about it."

B. They sat at the table. Mike told her that he had been asked by the student council president to run. "I think they had a wide choice of candidates. But they selected me. They think I would *surely* win." "I'm *glad* they wanted you, Mike. But don't be too sure of yourself," Mrs. Campbell cautioned. "There are four other candidates, but I'm sure I have a good *chance* to win,'" Mike repeated. He was excited.

C. From the moment his name had been placed on the ballot, Mike was constantly on a *merry-go-round*. "You should go to bed earlier," Mrs. Campbell would tell her son. "You haven't eaten supper with your family lately," Mr. Campbell remarked. "I would slow down if I could, dad. But this is important. Things progress quickly. I can't let my opponents get ahead of me," Mike replied to the admonish-

---

yelled: screamed
running for: being in a race
surely: certainly
glad: pleased
chance: opportunity
placed: put
merry-go-round: coming and going
anyway: anyhow
promise: assure
smile: grin
change: become different
campaign: work in the election
neat: elegant, nice
puzzled: confused

suddenly: unexpectedly
speech: talk
stage: platform
stated: said
continued: went on
common: everyone's
upcoming: next, future
responsibilities: duties
wished: wanted
following: next
returned: came back
voted: decided
voice: choice
agree: be satisfied

ments of his parents. "*Anyway,* I will rest when it's all over, I *promise,*" he added with a *smile.*

D. "If only he would dress this way all the time," Mrs. Campbell said at breakfast time. A complete *change* had come over Mike's dressing habits. Coat and tie were his daily attire during the *campaign.* In the past, he would never be seen in a tie at school. "I'll impress people as a *neat* dresser," he said, noticing the *puzzled* looks around the breakfast table. "Will I win the election, father?" Mike asked *suddenly.* "I'll prepare a good *speech.* Will you listen to it?" "Of course, son, we'll all listen to your speech. If you can convince us, you'll convince your fellow students." Mr. Campbell knew how to encourage Mike.

E. The election day came. It hasn't been easy for Mike to prepare his speech. "Yours is the best speech I've heard in years!" Mrs. Campbell exclaimed. "It may sound good here, but wait till I stand on the *stage,* in front of the entire student body. My teeth will be making so much noise, you won't be able to hear what I say!" Mike was really concerned. "You'll say it forcefully, Mike the way it should be said," Mr. Campbell said. "I can hardly wait to hear it." Mrs. Campbell remarked, "I'll be at school tomorrow to listen."

F. Mrs. Campbell proudly listened to her son's words. "Each president must dutifully maintain a working communication between the students and the administration," Mike *stated.* "We have a good school here," he *continued.* "With the cooperation of a concerned administration we should be able to accomplish a *common* goal in the *upcoming* school year. If our requests are sensible, I'm sure that the response will likewise be sensible." Mike paused.

G. "I say to you that I am aware of my *responsibilities* and shall be fully accountable for my actions. If I am elected, the student council will strive to achieve common goals with the administration. This I pledge to you. Thank you."

H. Mike finished his election speech. There was applause. Someone asked Mrs. Campbell, "Was that your son?" "Yes, that's my son!" Mrs. Campbell proudly replied. The friend said. "He delivered a fine speech. I hope he'll win." "So do I," Mrs. Campbell said.

I. It was not as the Campbells had *wished*. The *following* day, Mike *returned* home looking sad. "And he wasn't even the best man!" he exclaimed. "My speech was better than any of theirs!" Mike was close to tears. "You shouldn't take it this hard Mike," Mr. Campbell said. "Think of how much you've learned from it." "Still," Mike insisted, "I can't help but think that something is wrong when candidates get elected on popularity rather than on qualifications." "The students *voted*, Mike. The vote is the *voice* of the people in our system," Mr. Campbell added. "Well, I don't *agree* with the way the elections are held," Mike said stubbornly. "Some day, I'll work to change that."

Idea Questions:

1. How did Mrs. Campbell sense something unusual?

2. Why was Mike excited?

3. Why couldn't Mike slow down?

4. How did Mike change his ways?

5. Why was it important to write a good speech?

6. Do you think Mike's parents were helpful?

7. Did Mike express good ideas in his speech?

8. Why wasn't Mike elected president?

9. Why was Mike sad?

10. Can you tell the MAIN IDEA of this story?

Drawing of paragraph A & B

II *Words in Context [Pictographs]*

Below are some of the words used in the narrative. Where possible, each word has a [synonym], or it is defined as used in the story. Where possible, an *(antonym)* is also given. Make up sentences about the pictographs choosing the words you need. Read aloud.

Example: *(council)*= Mike was selected by the student council.

A. and B.

council [**planning body**]; sense [**feel**] *(ignore)*; good behavior [**good conduct**] *(misbehavior)*; suggest [**hint**] *(declare)*; wide [**broad**] *(narrow)*; choice [**many to pick from**] *(limited selection)*; candidate

Drawing of paragraph C & D

[**nominee**];select [**pick**] *(ignore, overlook)*; sure [**certain**] *(uncertain)*; caution [**warn**] (disregard); win [**get**] (lose)

C. and D.

ballot [**voting sheet**]; constant [**always**] *(seldom)*; lately [**recently**] *(long ago)*; remark [**notice**] *(disregard)*; slow down [**ease up**] *(speed up)*; important [**significant**] *(insignificant)*; let [**allow**] *(refuse)*; opponent [**adversary**] *(friend)*; get ahead [**progress**] *(fall behind)*; admonish [**caution**] dress [**clothe**] *(undress)*; complete [**total**] *(incomplete)*; habit [**custom**] attire [dress] *(bareness)*; impress [**affect**] *(undo)*; notice [**pay attention**] *(ignore)*; prepare [**fix**]; convince [**persuade**] *(dissuade)*; encourage [**support**] *(discourage)*

Drawing of paragraphs E, F & G

E., F. and G.

sound [**seem**]; in front of [**before**] *(behind)*; entire [**whole**] *(partial)* noise [**clamor**] *(stillness)*; concerned [**nervous**] *(indifferent)*; forceful [**powerful**] *(weak)*; proudly [**with pride**] *(humbly)*; duty [**responsibility**] *(freedom)*; maintain [**keep**] *(drop)*; communicate [**exchange ideas**]; continue [**persist**] *(cease)*; cooperate [**work together**] *(oppose)* accomplish [**achieve**] *(give up)*; request [**proposal**] *(command)*; conscious of [**realistic**] *(unrealistic)*; response [**reply**]; likewise [**also**] *(otherwise)*; aware [**sensible**] *(unaware)*; accountable [**responsible**] *(irresponsible)*; strive [**labor**] *(loaf)*; achieve [**accomplish**] *(fail)*; pledge [**promise**] *(refuse)*

H. and I.

finish [**end**] *(start)*; applause [**acclamation**]; deliver [**give**] *(take)*; fine [**good**] *(bad)*; close [**near**] *(far)*; hard [**difficult to bear**] *(easygoing)*; insist [**maintain**] *(yield)*; popular [**favorite**] *(unpopular)*; qualification [**capability**] *(inability)*; system [**order**] *(disorder)*; stubborn [**obstinate**] *(docile)*; change [**alter**] *(retain)*

III. Structures [Phrases]

Below are some phrases taken from the narrative. Make complete sentences and read them aloud.

1.	something		—unusual	—be
2.	at	—sit	—the	—table
3.	by	—ask	—the	—student council
4.	a	—have	—wide	—choice
5.	a	—have	—good	—change
6.	of	—help	—his	—parents
7.	his	—neat	—daily	—attire
8.	during		—the	—campaign
9.	it		—may	—sound good
10.	in		—front of	—the entire

IV. Sentences

A. Read the following sentences aloud. Repeat, substituting, where possible, with the synonym of the word in *italics*, or phrase that explains the meaning of the word. Make other necessary changes.

Example: His *conduct* changed.
            His *behavior* was different.

1. We will *proceed* with *care*.

2. You won't *hear* any *noise*.

3. Mike was really *concerned.*

4. You'll say it *forcefully.*

5. Mrs. Campbell *proudly* listened to Mike's words

6. We should be able to *accomplish* a common goal.

7. The *response* will be sensible.

8. I am aware of my *duties.*

9. I shall be *accountable* for my actions.

10. I *pledge* this to you.

11. Mike *finished* his election speech.

12. He *delivered* a fine speech.

13. Mike was *close* to tears.

14. It was *hard* to lose.

15. Mike *maintained* that something was wrong.

16. The students voted for their *favorite* candidate.

17. The *method* of voting was wrong.

18. Some day I'll work to *change* that.

B. Fill in the blanks with words from the narrative. Each space filled may be filled by a word or phrase. Do not refer back to the narrative. Where possible, use variations of the missing words. Read aloud.

Mike _____ never_____ this excited _____. "I'm _____ for president!" he _____. Mrs. Campbell_____ something_____. They _____at the table. Mike _____ her that he _____ asked to _____. They had a _____ choice of _____. But they _____ Mike. "I have a _____ chance to _____," Mike _____.

His name _____ placed on the _____. Mike was on a _____. His mother told him to show _____. "I can't _____ my _____ get_____ of me," Mike _____. "I will _____ when it's all _____."

"If only he _____ dress this way _____ the _____." Mrs. Campbell _____. A _____ change had come over Mike's _____ habits. In the _____ past he _____ never _____ in a tie at_____. "I'll _____ a good _____" Mike said. "If you _____ us, you'll convince your _____ students."

The _____ day came. It _____ been _____ for Mike. "Wait till I _____ on the _____ in front of the _____ student body!" Mike was _____. "You _____ say it _____," Mr. Campbell said. "I can_____ wait to _____ it." Mrs. Campbell remarked.

Mrs. Campbell _____ listened to her _____ speech. "We have a good _____," Mike said. "We should be _____ to _____ a common goal in the _____ school year. If our _____ are _____, I'm sure that the _____ will be _____ sensible."

"I am_____ of my _____ and shall be _____ for my _____ to you. If I am _____, we'll strive to _____ common goals with the _____." Mike _____ his _____ speech. There was _____.

The _____ day, Mike _____ home looking _____. "My speech was _____ than any of _____." "You shouldn't _____ it this _____ Mike," Mrs. Campbell said. "Think of how much you _____ learned from it." "The students _____, Mike. The _____ is the _____ of the _____ in our _____," Mr. Campbell added.

V. Grammar [Points of Interest]

A. The **Present Perfect** states something in the past that exists at the time of speaking. To form the *present perfect* we use the verb *have + past participle.*

Mike *has been asked* to run.
You *haven't eaten* supper with your family lately.
It *hasn't been* easy for Mike.
Think how much *you've learned* from it.

B. **Future Time**   *will, I'll* or *shall* + infinitive
   There is no verb to form the future tense as there was for the past
   tense. We will use the verb *will*, *'ll* or *shall* to express the future.
   This form also expresses

   1. *willingness*, or a *promise*, or an *agreement* with someone:
      Some day, *I'll work* to change that.
      I'll (I will) impress the people.
      I'll (I will) prepare a good speech.

   2. request:
      Will you *listen* to it?
      Will you please slow down?

   3. *questions* about the *future*:
      Will I *win* the election?
      Will you *help me?*

C. **Possessive Pronouns** are used in place of both a *possessive
   determiner* and a *noun*.

my son	=	*mine*	its son	=	*its*
your son	=	*yours*	our son	=	*ours*
his son	=	*his*	your son	=	*yours*
her son	=	*hers*	their son	=	*theirs*

   Was *my* speech good?
   Yours was the best.
   Yes, *mine* was better than *theirs*.

D. **Adverbials** answer the question words [**interrogatives**] *where?*
   (place), **how?** (manner), **when?** (time) of action. *Adverbs* are the
   most common adverbials.

   1. Place [**where?**]

      They sat *at the table.*
      He never wore a tie *at school.*

It sounds good *here.*
It will be different *on the stage.*
We have a good school *here.*

2. Manner [**how?**]

Most *adverbs of manner* are words that describe.
  (adjectives) + *-ly*

You haven't eaten supper with your family *lately.*
Mike dressed *neatly* during elections.
I can *hardly* wait to hear it.
Mrs. Campbell listened *proudly.*

Some *adverbs of manner* do not end in *-ly.*
  Things progress *fast.*

3. Time [**when?**]

The adverb of *time* is usually last, but it can begin a sentence when there is more than one adverb present.

TIME	PLACE	MANNER
Tomorrow	on the freeway	he'll drive slowly.
Last night	at school	he spoke carefully.

E. Uses of Modal Auxiliaries

1. We have used the auxiliary *would* in the sense of *be willing to,*
    If only wish he *would* dress this way all the time.

2. We have used the auxiliary *should* to express

a. *advisability:*
   You *should* go to bed earlier.
   You *shouldn't* take it this hard.

b. *expectation:*
   We *should* be able to accomplish a common end.

VI. Word Recognition

A. Circle the word (phrase) in Column II most *like* the word in Column I, and the word (phrase) in Column III most *unlike* the word in Column I. This oral identification of words ought to be timed.

COLUMN I	COLUMN II	COLUMN III
1. **accomplish**	a. achieve b. maintain c. sustain	a. fail b. demand c. think
2. **concerned**	a. forceful b. nervous c. powerful	a. humble b. indifferent c. weak
3. **duty**	a. responsibility b. behavior c. labor	a. choice b. attire c. freedom
4. **finish**	a. deliver b. end c. liberate	a. confine b. start c. fine
5. **get ahead**	a. progress faster b. prepare c. fix	a. fall behind b. admonish c. warn

6. **hard**

a. difficult to bear
b. insistent
c. persistent

a. easygoing
b. sensible
c. bad

7. **impress**

a. notice
b. mark
c. affect

a. undo
b. neglect
c. undress

8. **let**

a. ease up
b. be quick
c. allow

a. refuse
b. be glad
c. be pleased

9. **place**

a. put
b. suggest
c. hint

a. win
b. remove
c. declare

10. **popular**

a. right
b. firm
c. favorite

a. unpopular
b. bad
c. wrong

B. Pick the right expression. Complete the following sentences with the term that best fits the situation. Read aloud.

qualification	rest	select
permit	conscious	slow down
deliver	suddenly	suggest
impress	wide	forceful
concerned	duty	response
strive	accomplish	pledge

1. A person who does too many things at once needs to _____.

2. If a person has the capability, we say he has_____.

3. If a good book can affect you, it can _____ you.

4. Someone who is nervous may be _____.

5. Anytime you hint at something, you _____.

6. If something happen abruptly, we say it happens_____.

7. When there is a broad range of candidates, we say the choice is _____.

8. Anytime we wish to achieve a goal, we want to _____ it.

9. When Mike said his opponent was powerful, he meant he was _____.

10. You give someone a gift but you _____ a speech.

C. In the space on the left, write the word(s) that best fit the expression in bold print. Make other necessary changes. Read aloud.

_____ 1. Mrs. Campbell sensed something unusual in her son's *conduct*.

_____ 2. They had a wide *option* of candidates.

_____ 3. They *elected* me.

_____ 4. I think I'll *certainly* win.

_____ 5. I'm *pleased* they want you.

_____ 6. His name had been *put* on the ballot.

_____ 7. You haven't eaten your *evening meal*.

_____ 8. I would *ease* up if I could.

_____ 9. This is *pressing*.

_____ 10. I can't *permit* my *adversary* to get ahead.

_____ 11. His parents *warned* him.

_____ 12. A change came over his dressing *customs*.

_____ 13. Mike asked his father *abruptly*.

_____ 14. If you *persuade* us you'll *persuade* them.

_____ 15. Mrs. Campbell knew how to *support* Mike.

_____ 16. He stood in front of the *whole* student body.

_____ 17. It is our *obligation* to communicate.

_____ 18. Our *demands* are sensible.

_____ 19. The *reply* will be *also* sensible.

_____ 20. I will *labor* to gain the goals.

_____ 21. He *rendered* a fine speech.

_____ 22. He looked *sorrowful*.

_____ 23. I want to get elected on my *capability*.

_____ 24. This election *method* is wrong.

_____ 25. Mike was *obstinate*.

VII. Concept Recognition

Fill in the most appropriate word (phrase) to express the CONCEPT of the sentence according to the narrative. Read the complete sentence aloud.

A. Mike came home earlier than usual because he was_____ for president of the student body.
    1. yelling   3. running
    2. going   4. having

B. Mrs. Campbell suggested a cola because she _____.
    1. sensed something unusual   3. was in a hurry
    2. liked a drink   4. Mike was sad

C. Mike was glad that he was the _____ of the student council.
    1. president   3. choice
    2. student   4. name

D. Mike was sure he'd win, but Mrs. Campbell _____ him.
    1. reassured   3. excited
    2. cautioned   4. reminded

E. Mike was on a merry-go-round because things _____.
    1. slowdown   3. go well
    2. are important   4. progressed fast

F. Mike refused to listen to his parents' admonishments saying he'd rest
when _____.
   1. it's all over   3. he wins the election
   2. he loses the election   4. his opponent wins

G. The candidate dressed in coat and tie to _____ the students.
   1. notice   3. impress
   2. change   4. campaign

H. Mike prepared a good _____ to _____ the students.
   1. dress, please   3. quiz, ask
   2. speech, convince   4. dinner, win

I. Everyone in the Campbell family _____ Mike.
   1. liked   3. convinced
   2. prepared   4. encouraged

J. Mike worked hard on his speech to _____ the election.
   1. win   3. prepare
   2. convince   4. complete

K. Mike said in his speech that there must be _____ between the
students and administration.
   1. election   3. communication
   2. work   4. continuation

L. A common end can be accomplished if the administration is _____.
   1. common   3. upcoming
   2. concerned   4. able

M. Only _____ requests bring _____ response.
   1. good, better   3. common, upcoming
   2. sensible, sensible   4. concerned, common

N. Mike was sad because he lost and he thought _____.
    1. he was a better candidate   3. the other candidate was better
    2. no candidate was good   4. he didn't speak well

O. Mike thought the system of electing candidates on _____ rather than on qualification was _____.
    1. popularity, wrong   3. cooperation, right
    2. work, good   4. dressing, wrong

VIII Telling the Meaning

A. Place a check mark (✔) in front of the word in COLUMN II that best fits the MEANING of the word in COLUMN I. Read aloud a complete sentence using this word.

COLUMN I	COLUMN II

1. **abruptly**
    _____ a. suddenly
    _____ b. gradually
    _____ c. promptly

2. **accident**
    _____ a. caution
    _____ b. chance
    _____ c. plan

3. **accountable**
    _____ a. weak
    _____ b. responsible
    _____ c. irresponsible

4. **achieve**
    _____ a. give up
    _____ b. accomplish
    _____ c. cooperate

5. **affect**
    _____ a. notice
    _____ b. impress
    _____ c. undo

6. **capability**
   _____ a. method
   _____ b. incapability
   _____ c. qualification

7. **caution**
   _____ a. care
   _____ b. ability
   _____ c. recklessness

8. **complete**
   _____ a. incomplete
   _____ b. total
   _____ c. sensible

9. **concerned**
   _____ a. indifferent
   _____ b. nervous
   _____ c. sensible

10. **constant**
    _____ a. accountable
    _____ b. always
    _____ c. seldom

11. **convince**
    _____ a. dissuade
    _____ b. persuade
    _____ c. encourage

12. **early**
    _____ a. soon
    _____ b. late
    _____ c. wide

13. **front**
    _____ a. face
    _____ b. back
    _____ c. part

14. **get ahead**
    _____ a. progress faster
    _____ b. get behind
    _____ c. admonish

15. hint

_____ a. say
_____ b. declare
_____ c. suggest

16. important

_____ a. significant
_____ b. unimportant
_____ c. complete

B. Recognize words in the Narrative.

1. Which word in paragraph A. means "adversary"? _____

2. Which word in paragraph A. means "being in a race"? _____

3. Which word in paragraph B. means "good conduct"? _____

4. Which word in paragraph B. means "many to pick from"? _____

5. Which word in paragraph C. means "merry-go-round"? _____

6. Which word in paragraph D. means "become different"? _____

7. Which word in paragraph D. means "affect"? _____

8. Which word in paragraph E. means "whole"? _____

9. Which word in paragraph F. means "with pride"? _____

10. Which word in paragraph F. means "achieve"? _____

11. Which word in paragraph G. means "duty"? _____

12. Which word in paragraph H. means "acclamation"? _____

13. Which word in paragraph H. means "give"? _____

14. Which word in paragraph I. means "maintain"? _____

15. Which word in paragraph I. means "order"? _____

C. Return to Exercise A. Place two check marks (✔✔) in front of the word in COLUMN II that is the ANTONYM of the word in COLUMN I. Read aloud a complete sentence using this word.

D. Select one of the three (3) words (phrases) that best fulfills the MEANING of the sentence according to the narrative. Insert the word in the blank space.

1. Mike was excited because he was_____ for president of the student body.
   a. running   b. voting   c. unusual

2. The student council had a wide choice of candidates, but they _____ Mike.
   a. told   b. selected   c. repeated

3. Mike was sure of winning, but Mrs. Campbell _____ him.
   a. excited   b. selected   c. cautioned

4. When he ran for president, Mike was constantly_____.
   a. on a merry-   b. excited   c. slow
      go-round

5. Mike could not_____ because things_____ fast.
   a. slowdown,   b. understand it,   c. rest well,
      progressed   got   went

6. Mike promised to _____ when it was all over.
   a. vote   b. smile   c. rest

7. He dressed in coat and tie to _____ people.
   a. see   b. impress   c. win

8. The Campbells listened to Mike's speech to see if he could _____ them.
   a. fool   b. tell   c. convince

9. Mr. Campbell said a speech should be done_____.
   a. forcefully   b. concerned   c. easy

10. To accomplish a common goal, the requests should be
    a. good   b. common   c. sensible

11. When Mike returned home he was sad because he _____.
    a. wasn't the   b. was a better   C. he didn't win
    best man   man than his
                           opponent

IX. Comprehension [Exercises]

A. Place a check mark (✔) in front of the correct response to each of the statements according to the narrative. Read the complete sentences aloud.

1. Mike was excited because
   _____ a. he was elected president.
   _____ b. he was running for president.
   _____ c. he came home earlier than usual.

2. Mrs. Campbell suggested a cola to
   _____ a. learn more about Mike's candidacy.
   _____ b. practice Mike's speech.
   _____ c. make a speech.

3. Mike was glad that he was
   _____ a. having a cola.
   _____ b. talking to his mother.
   _____ c. selected out of a wide choice of candidates.

4. Mike was sure
_____ a. he had a good chance to win.
_____ b. he would win.
_____ c. he wouldn't win.

5. Mike could not slow down because
_____ a. his opponents were ahead of him.
_____ b. things progressed fast.
_____ c. his parents admonished him.

6. Mike promised to slow down when
_____ a. he won the election.
_____ b. ate supper.
_____ c. it was all over.

7. Mike dressed in coat and tie to
_____ a. win the election.
_____ b. impress people.
_____ c. make a complete change.

8. It was important for Mike to prepare a good speech to
_____ a. convince his fellow students.
_____ b. convince his family.
_____ c. convince himself.

9. Mike thought he would be frightened when
_____ a. the election came.
_____ b. he faced the student body.
_____ c. he faced his family.

10. To be a good president, one must
_____ a. be a good student.
_____ b. listen to the administration.
_____ c. maintain a working communication.

11. Mike was aware of

_____ a. the presidency.

_____ b. his responsibilities.

_____ c. his election.

12. Mike pledged to

_____ a. strive to achieve common goals.

_____ b. become the president.

_____ c. have action.

13. Mike was sad and close to tears because

_____ a. his speech was better.

_____ b. his opponent's speech was good.

_____ c. the winner wasn't the best man.

14. Mike felt that the candidates were

_____ a. elected on popularity.

_____ b. elected fairly.

_____ c. better speakers than he.

B. Below there are three (3) different thoughts in each of the exercises. Assign the proper sequence (order) of THOUGHT, according to the narrative by numbering 1 to 3. Read aloud.

1. a. excited before _____

   b. never been this _____

   c. Mike had _____

2. a. earlier than usual _____

   b. home from school _____

   c. he came _____

3. a. in her son's behavior _____

   b. Mrs. Campbell sensed _____

   c. something unusual _____

4. a. choice of candidates _____
   b. they had a wide _____
   c. I think _____

5. a. get ahead of me _____
   b. let my opponents _____
   c. I can't _____

6. a. I promise _____
   b. when it's all over _____
   c. I'll rest _____

7. a. all the time _____
   b. dress this way _____
   c. if only he would _____

8. a. Mike's dressing habits _____
   b. a complete change _____
   c. came over _____

9. a. in the past _____
   b. seen in a tie at school _____
   c. he would never be _____

10. a. Mrs. Campbell _____
    b. to encourage Mike _____
    c. knew how _____

11. a. to prepare his speech _____
    b. easy for Mike _____
    c. it hadn't been _____

12. a. it should be said _____
    b. forcefully, Mike, the way _____
    c. you'll say it _____

13. a. to her son's words   _____
   b. proudly listened   _____
   c. Mrs. Campbell   _____

14. a. the students and the administration   _____
   b. a working communication between   _____
   c. each president must dutifully maintain   _____

15. a. if our requests are sensible   _____
   b. response will be likewise sensible   _____
   c. I'm sure that the   _____

16. a. goals with the administration   _____
   b. will strive to achieve common   _____
   c. if I am elected I   _____

17. a. any of theirs   _____
   b. better than   _____
   c. my speech was   _____

18. a. the vote is the voice   _____
   b. in our system   _____
   c. of the people   _____

19. a. to change that   _____
   b. some day   _____
   c. I'll work   _____

C. There are some statements listed below about the narrative.
Write **T** for **True** in front of each statement that you think is true.
Write **F** for **False** if the statement is not true. Read aloud.

_____ 1. Mike was always excited.

_____ 2. He came home earlier than usual.

_____ 3. He spoke calmly to his mother.

_____ 4. Mrs. Campbell suggested a cola.

_____ 5. Mike told his mother he was president of the student body.

_____ 6. Mrs. Campbell cautioned her son.

_____ 7. Mike thought he had a good chance to win.

_____ 8. Mike went to sleep late.

_____ 9. He always ate supper with the family.

_____ 10. Mike was going to rest when he won.

_____ 11. Mike's dressing habits changed.

_____ 12. The Campbells listened to Mike's speech.

_____ 13. Mrs. Campbell didn't encourage her son.

_____ 14. It was easy for Mike to prepare his speech.

_____ 15. Mike said that there must be many requests.

_____ 16. He said that he was aware of his responsibilities.

_____ 17. He also said that he would strive to achieve common goals with the administration.

_____ 18. The following day Mike returned home happy.

_____ 19. The vote is the voice of the people.

_____ 20. Mike agreed with the way elections were held.

_____ 21. He promised to change the system.

X. Composition and Discussion

A. In COLUMN I are the beginnings of sentences. In COLUMN II are
the completions to sentences of COLUMN I. Select the completion
best fitting each sentence in COLUMN I according to the narrative.
Read the completed sentences orally. Compose new sentences orally
and discuss the narrative.

<table>
<tr><th>COLUMN I</th><th>COLUMN II</th></tr>
<tr><td>1. Mike had never been</td><td>a. as the Campbells had wished.</td></tr>
<tr><td>2. He came home from school</td><td>b. this way all the time.</td></tr>
<tr><td>3. They sat</td><td>c. on a merry-go-round.</td></tr>
<tr><td>4. I think they had</td><td>d. a good speech.</td></tr>
<tr><td>5. Mike was constantly</td><td>e. earlier than usual.</td></tr>
<tr><td>6. I would slow down</td><td>f. at the table.</td></tr>
<tr><td>7. I will rest</td><td>g. if I could.</td></tr>
<tr><td>8. If only he would dress</td><td>h. this excited before.</td></tr>
<tr><td>9. A complete change</td><td>i. for Mike to prepare his speech.</td></tr>
<tr><td>10. I'll impress people</td><td>j. tomorrow to listen.</td></tr>
<tr><td>11. I'll prepare</td><td>k. as a neat dresser.</td></tr>
<tr><td>12. Mrs. Campbell knew</td><td>l. when it's all over.</td></tr>
<tr><td>13. It hadn't been easy</td><td>m. how to encourage Mike.</td></tr>
<tr><td>14. I'll be at school</td><td>n. a wide choice of candidates.</td></tr>
<tr><td>15. We have a</td><td>o. came over Mike's dressing habits.</td></tr>
<tr><td>16. It was not</td><td>p. good school here.</td></tr>
</table>

B. 1. Tell us about an election.

2. Tell us about Mike's speech.

3. How did the Campbells help Mike?

4. Why did Mike feel sad?

5. Describe the change in Mike's behavior.

C. Describe what you see in the picture below.

D. Read the poem aloud. Answer, orally, the questions listed following
the poem.

A Question

His life has gone with the winds of forgotten days.   [1] force
He will dream of none but the final truth.   [2] shake
He will seek a might [1] *that trembles* [2] *not nor sways* [3]   [3] affect
That knows no aging transition [4] *from youth...*   [4] change

This force has no end such as this, for it had no beginning.
Can there be something greater? Tell me! Do!   [5] judged
Or is my very question condemned [5] *for a sin?*   [6] image
Is there an idol [6] *image more splendid* [7] *than truth?*   [7] magnificent

Scorn [8] *not the dying for asking reply* [9]
To questions he has blindly accepted before.   [8] ridicule
He shall die seeking. [10] *His work is done.*   [9] answer
Soon he will find the answer at last...   [10] searching

1. Identify present perfect sentences.
2. Identify future time sentences.
3. Identify sentences containing modal auxiliaries.
4. Does the title express the idea of the entire poem?
5. In which verse lies the expression of a promise?

CHAPTER SIX

THE ENCHANTED MOUNTAIN

IN THIS CHAPTER

Words to remember:

Past Perfect Tense
had + past participle

Comparison = equal things
unequal things

very, too, so, + **Adjective (Adverb)**
and + too - and + so - but

I. Narrative

A. Little Lucy was *unable* to explain why she had climbed the mountain to the very top. Had she been able to understand what had happened, she might have *explained* it to those who asked. As it was, as often as she tried, things got too involved. She decided instead to tell the *entire* story.

B. That morning, it was very foggy, and Lucy *lost her way* completely. Before she knew how it had happened, she was *at the foot* of a huge green mountain. She had gone too far. There was no one there, but Lucy was not afraid. On the contrary, she became very curious and was too excited to think of danger. It seemed so easy to climb that Lucy *looked forward to* her *ascent* with great anticipation.

C. When she had reached the very *top*, she was suddenly surrounded by a throng of small creatures. They were taller than herself, but they were shapeless and colorless. Many *bathed* in the clear water of the immense lake. She had never seen such creatures before. Nor had she

---

enchanted: charmed
unable: incapable (of+ v-ing)
explained: make clear
entire: whole
lost her way: got confused
at the foot: at the bottom
looked forward to: was eager
ascent: going up
top: the highest part
bathed: washed
withdraw: go back, away
presence: being there
noticed: observed
stepped up: walked over
closer: nearer
welcome: thanks for coming

no end: very much
response: answer
amazement: puzzlement
paused: stopped
lake: large body of water
below: lower place
concluded: decided
hurt: cause pain, injure
caught: understood
repeaters: someone who does
    something again
push: shove, force
over: down
else: different, more
gone: disappeared
left: alone, by herself

been told they existed. It was too late for her to *withdraw*. Her *presence* was *noticed*, and she was afraid to move from the spot.

D. Lucy was very frightened, and so were the little creatures. She remembered vaguely someone had told her that fear is caused by the unknown. Lucy smiled, and so did the faces of the little shapeless, colorless creatures. One of them, he seemed as frightened as the rest, *stepped up closer* to the girl.

E. "*Welcome* to the Enchanted Mountain, Lucy," he said in perfect English, which surprised the little girl to *no end*. "We are the Erutuf people," the creature continued, as though in *response* to Lucy's mute *amazement*. "We live on this mountain. Our ancestors have been its inhabitants before us." He *paused* for a moment. "You see the Erutuf bathing in the *lake below*? They're being punished for spreading gossip, for being greedy, and for being envious of other Erutuf people."

F. "Is taking a bath punishment?" Lucy exclaimed. "It is, if you don't like taking a bath. We are known for that. We hate water!" the Erutuf cried louder than she had ever heard anyone cry. "Three baths daily are more than anyone can stand," he *concluded* seriously. Lucy was silent. She was too afraid to *hurt* the little creature's feelings.

G. "But how could anyone be prejudiced in this place, among creatures without color and without shape?" Lucy asked without saying a word. Again, the little Erutuf *caught* her silent inquiry. "You'll be surprised to hear this, Lucy, but we do very simple things here. The simpler, the better. And what's simpler than hate and bigotry?" "Love!" Lucy replied quickly. "Do they love where you come from?" the Erutuf asked. Lucy didn't know how to answer that. She kept silent.

H. "We found a way to punish the incorrigibles more severely than the mere *repeaters*. They are given color and shape. Then, they are banished from the top to the mountainside. From there, they must work their way up to the top for thirteen years. When they become colorless and shapeless again, they are accepted in our community. And all the time refuse is their food. We *push* that *over* the side too. There's nothing *else* they can eat."

I. "I wish to leave this place right now!" Lucy cried. "I want to go home to my family. Please, let me go! You are more cruel than anyone I know. Even Miss Conklin, the history teacher!" At the first sight of tears, even quicker than you could say "Erutuf," the little creatures were all *gone*. The bathers were gone too. Only Lucy was *left*, her eyes closed, alone and no longer frightened.

J. When she opened her eyes, she was with her family. There was a look of concern on her parents' faces. Lucy sensed that something had happened. She knew that she would have to explain. Grown-ups always want things explained. But as hard as she tried, Lucy was unable to explain. She decided then it would be better to draw them a picture. Someday, she would do this, not just now.

Idea Questions:

1. Why did Lucy decide to tell the story?

2. Why did Lucy want to climb the mountain?

3. Why was Lucy frightened?

4. How did the Erutuf people amaze Lucy?

5. Why didn't Lucy run away?

6. Do you think taking a bath is punishment? Why? Why not?

7. Do you think telling gossip is wrong? Why? Why not?

8. Do you think being greedy is wrong? Why? Why not?

9. Do you think greed and gossip ought to be punished? Why? Why not?

10. Can you tell about the MAIN IDEA of this story?

II. Words in Context [Pictographs]

Below are some of the words used in the narrative. Where possible, each word has a *[synonym]*, or it is defined as used in the story. Where possible, an *(antonym)* is also given. Make up sentences about the pictographs choosing the words you need. Read aloud.

Example: [ascend] = She ascended the mountain.

A. and B.

explain *[tell clearly] (obscure)* ; climb *[ascend] (descend)* ; mountain *[large hill] (valley)* ; top *[summit] (bottom)* ; involved *[confused, intricate] (simple)* ; decide *[determine]* (doubt); instead *[in place of]* ; foggy *[misty] (clear)* ; completely *[entirely] (not at all)* ; huge *[enormous] (diminutive)* ; contrary *[opposite]* ; curious *[inquiring] (indifferent)* ; danger *[peril] (safety)* ; forward *[ahead] (backward)* ; anticipation *[expectation] (misapprehension)*

Drawing of paragraph A & B

Drawing of paragraph C & D

C. and D.

reach *[arrive at]* *(revert)* ; suddenly *[abruptly]* *(gradually)* ; surround *[encircle]* ; throng *[crowd]* ; creature *[being]* ; tall *[high]* *(short)* ; shapeless *[formless]* *(formed)* ; colorless *[lacking hue]* *(colorful)* ; clear *[transparent]* *(muddy)*; immense *[enormous]* *(tiny)* ; exist *[live]* *(die)* ; move *[stir]* *(rest)* ; spot *[place]* ; vaguely *[indefinitely]* *(definitely)* ; unknown *[unfamiliar]* *(known)*

Drawing of paragraphs E, F & G

E. F. and G.

enchanted *[charmed]* *(disenchanted)* ; perfect *[faultless]* *(imperfect)*;
amazed *[surprised]* *(unamazed)* ; ancestor *[forebear]* *(descendant)* ;
inhabitant *[occupant]* ; punish *[chastise]* *(reward)*; spread *[circulate]* ;
gossip *[spread rumor]* *(be discrete)* ; greedy *[avaricious]* *(generous)* ; envious *[jealous]* *(satisfied)* ; hate *[detest]* *(love)* ; loud *[noisy]* *(quiet)* ; stand
[tolerate] ; prejudice *[bigotry]* *(fairness)* ; inquiry *[question]* *(statement)* ;
surprise *[astonish]* *(forewarn)* ; simple *[uncomplicated]* *(complicated)*

Drawing of paragraphs E, F & G

H. I. and J.

incorrigible *[hopeless]* *(hopeful)* ; severely *[harshly]* *(leniently)* ; banish *[exile]* *(shelter)* ; side *[edge]* *(center)* ; work *[labor]* *(rest)* ; community *[society]* *(disunity)* ; refuse *[garbage]* ; cruel *[inhuman]* *(humane)* ; sight *[seeing]* *(blindness)* ; try *[attempt]* *(abandon)*

III. Structures [Phrases]

Below are some PHRASES taken from the narrative. Make complete sentences and read them aloud.

1. unable	be	to	explain
2. to	climb	the	very top
3. as	try	she	unable

4. at	be	the	foot
5. so	be	easy	to climb
6. reached	she	the	very top
7. the	creatures	be	shapeless
8. move	can	from	the spot
9. cause	it	by	the unknown
10. closer	come	to	the girl
11. from	banish	the	top
12. up	come	to the	top

IV. Sentences

A. Read the following sentences aloud. Repeat, substituting where possible, the synonym of the words in *italics*, or a phrase that explains the meaning. Make other necessary changes.

Example: Lucy could not *clear up* the story.
Lucy was unable to *explain* the story.

1. She had seen a *huge* mountain.

2. They are *banished* from the top.

3. They must *work* their way up.

4. They had been *punished*.

5. *Refuse* is their food.

6. We had pushed that over the *side*.

7. There's nothing else the *community* can do.

8. I had *tried* to leave this place.

9. You are full of *prejudice*.

10. The little *creatures* were gone.

11. The bathers were very *loud*.

12. Only Lucy was *enchanted*.

13. She was no longer *involved*.

14. She *determined* to open her eyes.

15. She was out of great *peril*.

16. There was a look of *concern*.

17. Lucy *sensed* that something had happened.

18. She had to explain the *unfamiliar* place.

19. Lucy was *unable* to do it.

20. She had been *astonished*.

B. Fill in the blanks with words from the narrative. Each space may be filled by a word or phrase. Do not refer back to the narrative. Where possible, use variations of the missing words. Read aloud.

Lucy was unable to _____ why she _____ the mountain to the very _____. _____ she _____ able to _____ what happened, she might _____ explained it to _____ who _____.

On the _____ of the day it was _____ and Lucy lost her _____ completely. She was at the _____ of a _____ green _____. It _____ so easy to _____ that Lucy looked to her _____ with great _____.

When she _____ the very top, she _____ suddenly _____ by a _____ of small creatures. They were _____ than _____, but they were _____ and _____. She never _____ such creatures.

Lucy was _____, and so _____ the little _____. She _____ vaguely someone _____ her that fear is _____ by the _____. Lucy _____, and so did the _____ on the _____ shapeless, _____ creatures. One of _____ stepped up _____ to the girl.

"Welcome to the _____, Lucy," he said in _____ English. "We are the Erutuf _____," the _____ continued. "We live on this _____. Our

_____ been its inhabitants _____ us." He _____ for a moment. "The Erutuf bathing in the _____ are being _____ for _____ gossip."

"Is taking a _____ punishment?" Lucy _____ amazed. "It is, if you don't _____ taking a _____. We are _____ for that. We _____ water!" The Erutuf _____ louder _____ she _____ ever _____ anyone cry. "Three _____ daily are _____ than anyone can _____."

"But how could anyone be _____ in this place, creatures without _____ and without _____?" Lucy _____ without saying a _____. "You'll be _____ to hear this, Lucy, but we _____ very _____ things here. The _____, the _____. And what's _____ than _____ and _____?" "Love!" Lucy _____ quickly.

"We found a _____ to _____ the _____ more _____than the mere _____. They are given _____ and _____. Then, they are _____ from the _____ to the _____. From there, they must _____ their way _____ to the for thirteen _____. When they _____ colorless and _____ again, they are _____ in our community."

"I wish to _____ this _____ right now!" Lucy cried. "I want to go _____ to my _____!" At the _____ sight of _____, even _____ than you could say Erutuf, the _____ creatures were all _____. The _____ were _____ too.

When Lucy _____ her eyes, she was _____ her _____. She _____ that something _____ happened. She knew that she _____ have to _____. Grown-ups _____ want _____ explained.

V. Grammar (Points of Interest)

A. The *Past Perfect* refers to an event that happened before *another* event in the past. The other event is usually introduced by *when* or an expression that answers *when*. The past perfect also occurs in *dependent clauses*. The verb in the *main clause* is in the *past tense*. Sometimes the reverse is true.

Little Lucy was *unable* to explain why she had climbed the mountain.

She might *have explained* it, had she been able to understand.

She was suddenly *surrounded* when she had reached the top.

B. ***Comparison*** means to compare two equal things (as...as) or to compare two unequal things (*-er than or more than*).

    1.   Two *equal* things:

        As often *as* she tried, things got too involved.

        One of them seemed *as* much frightened *as* the rest.

        They're being punished for spreading gossip *as* well *as* for being envious.

        As hard *as* she tried, Lucy was unable to explain.

    2.   Two unequal things:

        The Erutuf cried *louder than* she had ever heard anyone cry.

        They were *taller than* Lucy.

        What's *simpler than* hate and bigotry?

        Punish them *more severely than* repeaters.

        Even *quicker than* you could say "Erutuf."

        It would be *better* to draw them a picture.

C. 1. Use the words *very, too, so* + Adjective (Adverb):

        Lucy became *very curious.*

        It was *very foggy* and she lost her way.

        Lucy was *very frightened.*

        We do the *very simple* things here.

She had gone *too far*.

It was *too late* for her to withdraw.

She was *too afraid* to hurt his feelings.

It was *so foggy* that she lost her way.

It seemed *so easy* to climb that Lucy looked forward to it.

2. Use of and + too:

    We are small, *and you are too*.

    Lucy was frightened, *and they were too*.

    We are punished, *and they are too*.

    The Erutuf cried, *and Lucy did too*.

3. Use of *and* + *so* :

    Lucy was frightened, *and so were* the little creatures.

    Lucy smiled, *and so did* the faces of the creatures.

    One of them stepped up closer, *and so did* the others.

    They're being punished, *and so are* the others.

4. Uses of *but*:

    Lucy wanted to explain, *but* she did not understand.

    There was no one there, *but* Lucy was not afraid.

    They were taller, *but* they were shapeless.

    You'll be surprised, *but* we do simple things here.

VI. Word Recognition

A. Circle the word in Column II most like the word in Column I, and the word in Column III most unlike the word in Column I. This oral identification of words ought to be timed.

COLUMN I	COLUMN II	COLUMN III
1. **completely**	a. entirely b. contrary c. adverse	a. favorable b. diminutive c. not at all
2. **cruel**	a. nice b. healthy c. inhumane	a. gentle b. humane c. loving
3. **danger**	a. curiosity b. peril c. inquiry	a. decision b. security c. misapprehension
4. **explain**	a. clear up b. involve c. implicate	a. decide b. determine c. obscure
5. **foggy**	a. entire b. whole c. misty	a. contrary b. clear c. opposite
6. **greedy**	a. avaricious b. unfamiliar c. jealous	a. loud b. familiar c. generous
7. **immense**	a. curious b. enormous c. crowded	a. tiny b. tall c. high

8. **incorrigible**

a. complex	a. generous
b. greedy	b. hopeful
c. hopeless	c. satisfied

9. **inquiry**

a. bias	a. statement
b. question	b. fairness
c. prejudice	c. love

10. **mountain**

a. top	a. valley
b. large hill	b. bottom
c. summit	c. forest

11. **open**

a. candid	a. simple
b. free	b. secretive
c. contrary	c. senseless

12. **perfect**

a. commonplace	a. disenchanted
b. faultless	b. complex
c. charmed	c. imperfect

13. **punish**

a. gossip	a. reward
b. spread rumor	b. be discrete
c. chastise	c. circulate

14. **reach**

a. move	a. revert
b. stir	b. rest
c. arrive at	c. clear

15. **severely**

a. loudly	a. leniently
b. noisily	b. quietly
c. harshly	c. slowly

B. Pick the right expression. Complete the following sentences with the term that best fits the situation. Read aloud.

gossip   side   suddenly
amazed   vaguely   enchanted
ancestor   shapeless hate
incorrigible   colorless severely
immense   exist   envious

1. If something is formless, we say it is _____.

2. Anytime a person is hopeless, we can say he is _____.

3. When you treat people harshly, you treat them _____.

4. When we say the mountain was charmed, we can say it was _____.

5. If you see something that's lacking hue, it is _____.

6. When you remember something indefinitely, you remember it _____.

7. Being jealous means that you are _____.

8. If you detest something, you _____ it.

9. To live means to _____.

10. Somebody who is surprised may be _____.

C. In the space on the left write the word(s) that best fit the expression in **bold print**. Make other necessary changes. Read aloud.

_____ 1. Lucy was unable to **tell clearly** why she climbed the montains.

_____ 2. She **determined** to tell the story.

_____ 3. It was very **foggy**.

_____ 4. She lost her way **entirely**.

_____ 5. Lucy was at the foot of a **huge** mountain.

_____ 6. She was too curious to think of **_peril_**.

_____ 7. She was **_suddenly surrounded_**.

_____ 8. There was a **_crowd_** of small creatures.

_____ 9. They were **_formless_**.

_____ 10. There was an **_enormous_** lake.

_____ 11. Lucy could not move from the **_spot_**.

_____ 12. This is the **_charmed_** mountain.

_____ 13. He spoke English to Lucy's **_astonishment_**.

_____ 14. Those in the lake were being **_chastised_**.

_____ 15. They were punished for being **_avaricious_**.

_____ 16. We **_detest_** water.

_____ 17. How could anyone be **_biased_** here?

_____ 18. You'll be **_astonished_** to hear this.

_____ 19. We do very **_uncomplicated_** things here.

_____ 20. She replied **_promptly_**.

_____ 21. We found a way to punish the **_hopeless_**.

_____ 22. They are punished more **_severely_**.

_____ 23. They are **_exiled_** from the top.

VII Concept Recognition

Fill in the most appropriate word (phrase) to express the CONCEPT of the sentence according to the narrative. Read the complete sentence aloud.

A. Little Lucy climbed to the top of the mountain, but she was unable to _____ it.

1. explain   3. involve
2. separate   4. implicate

B. She could not explain, because she was not able to _____ it herself.
1. decide
2. determine
3. understand
4. wave

C. Because it was foggy, Lucy had _____ her way.
1. cleared
2. lost
3. reached
4. grasped

D. Lucy was not _____, even though no one was there.
1. colorless
2. curious
3. lacking hue
4. afraid

E. Her excitement made her forget the _____.
1. danger
2. forestallment
3. anticipation
4. misapprehension

F. She looked forward to her ascent because it _____.
1. seemed easy
2. was contrary
3. was dangerous
4. was ahead

G. The creatures were small, but they were _____ than Lucy.
1. clearer
2. taller
3. more shapeless
4. colorless

H. She had never seen such creatures. She didn't know they _____.
1. existed
2. encircled
3. surrounded
4. missed

I. It was too late for her to withdraw because her _____ was _____.
1. throng, translucent
2. danger, known
3. presence, noticed
4. smile, unknown

J. Lucy was very _____, and so were the little creatures.
1. immense
2. definite
3. frightened
4. clear

K. Because someone had told her, she knew that was caused by the

_____.

1. fear, unknown   3. spot, known

2. throng, creatures   4. crowd, beings

L. When Lucy _____, the faces of the Erutuf _____ also.

1. talked, talked   3. reached, reached

2. smiled, smiled   4. moved, moved

M. Even though Lucy did not _____, the Erutuf knew what she wanted
to say.

1. speak   3. move

2. reach   4. liberate

N. The Erutuf people lived on the mountain because their _____ lived
there before them.

1. unknown   3. anonymous

2. throng   4. ancestors

O. Those Erutuf who bathed in the lake were being _____.

1. rewarded   3. loved

2. chastised   4. hated

P. Lucy was silent because she didn't want to _____ the little creature.

1. investigate   3. hurt

2. conjecture   4. love

Q. Lucy didn't understand how anyone could be _____ on the
mountain.

1. prejudiced   3. loved

2. hated   4. astonished

R. Lucy wanted to return home because she thought that the Erutuf
were _____.

1. prejudiced   3. biased

2. cruel   4. quiet

S. Lucy knew she would have to _____ because grown-ups want things _____.
  1. explain, explained
  2. hate, loved
  3. stand, simple
  4. punish, rewarded

VIII. Telling the Meaning

A. Place a check mark (✔) in front of the word in COLUMN II that best fits the MEANING of the word in COLUMN I. Read aloud a complete sentence using this word.

COLUMN I   COLUMN II

1. **abruptly**   _____ a. gradually
                       _____ b. completely
                       _____ c. suddenly

2. **arrive at**   _____ a. reach
                       _____ b. anticipate
                       _____ c. revert

3. **avaricious**   _____ a. unfamiliar
                       _____ b. greedy
                       _____ c. generous

4. **chastise**   _____ a. reward
                       _____ b. punish
                       _____ c. forewarn

5. **climb**   _____ a. descend
                       _____ b. ascend
                       _____ c. walk

6. **colorless**   _____ a. lacking hue
                       _____ b. clear
                       _____ c. colorful

7. **community**   _____ a. society
                          _____ b. feeling
                          _____ c. segregation

8. **completely**   _____ a. not at all
                          _____ b. entirely
                          _____ c. contrary

9. **curious**   _____ a. adverse
                          _____ b. indifferent
                          _____ c. inquiring

10. **danger**   _____ a. peril
                          _____ b. question
                          _____ c. security

11. **decide**   _____ a. doubt
                          _____ b. determine
                          _____ c. part

12. **enormous**   _____ a. tiny
                          _____ b. immense
                          _____ c. curious

13. **exist**   _____ a. die
                          _____ b. live
                          _____ c. move

14. **faultless**   _____ a. imperfect
                          _____ b. perfect
                          _____ c. charmed

15. **formless**   _____ a. formed
                          _____ b. high
                          _____ c. shapeless

16. **forward**

———— a. contrary
———— b. backward
———— c. ahead

17. **gossip**

———— a. be discrete
———— b. spread rumors
———— c. be jealous

B. Recognize words in the Narrative.

1. Which word in paragraph A. means "made clear"? ————————

2. Which word in paragraph A. means "incapable of"? ————————

3. Which word in paragraph B. means "misty"? ————————

4. Which word in paragraph B. means "got confused"? ————————

5. Which word in paragraph C. means "the highest point"? ————————

6. Which word in paragraph C. means "enormous"? ————————

7. Which word in paragraph D. means "indefinitely"? ————————

8. Which word in paragraph D. means "unfamiliar"? ————————

9. Which word in paragraph D. means "walked over"? ————————

10. Which word in paragraph E. means "forbear"? ————————

11. Which word in paragraph E. means "circulate"? ————————

12. Which word in paragraph F. means "chastise"? ————————

13. Which word in paragraph G. means "question"? ————————

14. Which word in paragraph H. means "exiled"? ————————

15. Which word in paragraph I. means "inhumane"? ————————

16. Which word in paragraph J. means "attempted"? ————————

C. Return to Exercise A. Place two check marks (✔✔) in front of the word in COLUMN II that is the ANTONYM of the word in COLUMN I. Read aloud a complete sentence using this word.

D. Select one of the three (3) words (phrases) that best fulfills the MEANING of the sentence according to the narrative. Insert the word in the blank space. Read the completed sentence aloud.

1. Lucy was unable to explain why she had climbed the mountain because she did not _____ it herself.
   a. understand   b. clear up   c. obscure

2. She tried many times to explain, but things got too _____.
   a. obscure   b. involved   c. separated

3. Lucy was not afraid because she became very _____.
   a. clear   b. excited   c. adverse

4. She looked forward to her ascent because it seemed _____ to climb.
   a. clear   b. contrary   c. easy

5. Lucy thought there was no one, but she was _____ by a throng of creatures.
   a. liberated   b. surrounded   c. formed

6. She wanted to withdraw, but she didn't _____ because her presence was noticed.
   a. stir   b. exist   c. die

7. She remembered that fear is caused by the _____ and she smiled.
   a. known   b. definite   c. unknown

8. Though Lucy didn't say a word, the little creatures _____ her questions.
   a. answered   b. declared   c. punished

9. The Erutuf people bathed in the lake because they were being _____.
   a. chastised   b. rewarded   c. hated

10. Lucy was silent because she didn't want to _____ the creature's feelings.

    a. love   b. hurt   c. prejudice

11. Though the Erutuf were colorless and shapeless, they were _____.

    a. kind   b. bigoted   c. fair

12. There was a way to punish the _____ by giving them color and shape.

    a. occupants   b. people   c. incorrigibles

13. Because they were being punished, the incorrigibles received _____ for food.

    a. fairness   b. love   c. refuse

14. Lucy knew she would have to explain because grown-ups _____ explained.

    a. refuse slow   b. see work   c. want things

IX. Comprehension [Exercises]

A. Place a check mark (✔) in front of the correct response to each of the statements according to the narrative. Read the complete sentence aloud.

1. Lucy was unable to explain why she had climbed the mountain because
    _____ a. she was afraid.
    _____ b. she didn't understand it herself.
    _____ c. she didn't want to.

2. She decided
    _____ a. to tell the whole story.
    _____ b. to get things involved.
    _____ c. to try.

3. Because it was very foggy, Lucy
   _____ a. climbed the mountain.
   _____ b. lost her way.
   _____ c. was afraid.

4. The mountain was
   _____ a. small and dark.
   _____ b. like a hill.
   _____ c. huge and green.

5. Lucy became curious and too excited
   _____ a. to climb the mountain.
   _____ b. to think of danger.
   _____ c. to go too far.

6. She looked forward to her ascent because
   _____ a. it seemed easy to climb.
   _____ b. it seemed difficult to climb.
   _____ c. it was clear.

7. When Lucy reached the top
   _____ a. she was alone.
   _____ b. she was at home.
   _____ c. she was surrounded by creatures.

8. The small creatures were
   _____ a. clear and known.
   _____ b. shapeless and colorless.
   _____ c. Lucy's friends.

9. Lucy did not withdraw because
   _____ a. she was tired.
   _____ b. her presence was noticed.
   _____ c. she liked the creatures.

10. When Lucy smiled,

_____ a. no one spoke to her.

_____ b. she was frightened.

_____ c. so did the faces of the little creatures.

11. The little creature

_____ a. welcomed Lucy.

_____ b. was surprised.

_____ c. was unfriendly.

12. The Erutuf people were punished for

_____ a. crying loudly.

_____ b. being greedy and envious.

_____ c. being kind.

13. The Erutuf people were punished

_____ a. by hating water.

_____ b. by loving water.

_____ c. by taking a bath.

14. The incorrigibles were punished when

_____ a. they talked with Lucy.

_____ b. they took a bath.

_____ c. they were given food.

15. The incorrigibles could return to their community when

_____ a. they loved one another.

_____ b. they became colorless and shapeless.

_____ c. they ate refuse.

16. Because Lucy was unable to explain, she decided

_____ a. to draw a picture.

_____ b. to climb the mountain.

_____ c. to take her parents to the mountain.

B. Below there are three (3) different thoughts in each of the exercises. Assign the proper sequence (order) of THOUGHT, according to the narrative, by numbering 1 to 3. Read aloud.

1. a. the mountain to the very top   _____
   b. why she had climbed   _____
   c. little Lucy was unable to explain   _____

2. a. the entire story   _____
   b. to tell   _____
   c. she decided instead   _____

3. a. on the morning of that day   _____
   b. it was very foggy and Lucy   _____
   c. lost her way completely   _____

4. a. was not afraid   _____
   b. there, but Lucy   _____
   c. there was no one   _____

5. a. it seemed so easy to climb   _____
   b. ascent with great anticipation   _____
   c. that Lucy looked forward to her   _____

6. a. shapeless and colorless   _____
   b. they were taller than   _____
   c. herself, but they were   _____

7. a. many bathed   _____
   b. of the immense lake   _____
   c. in the clear water   _____

8. a. to move from the spot   _____
   b. her presence was noticed,   _____
   c. and she was afraid   _____

9. a. the little creatures   _____
    b. and so were   _____
    c. Lucy was very frightened,   _____

10. a. someone had told her   _____
    b. she remembered vaguely   _____
    c. that fear is caused by the unknown   _____

11. a. the creature continued,   _____
    b. "We are the Erutuf people."   _____
    c. as though in response to Lucy's   _____
       mute amazement

12. a. before us   _____
    b. had been its inhabitants   _____
    c. our ancestors   _____

13. a. Lucy exclaimed,   _____
    b. a bath punishment?"   _____
    c. "is taking   _____

14. a. heard anyone cry   _____
    b. than she had ever   _____
    c. the Erutuf cried louder   _____

15. a. anyone can stand   _____
    b. daily are more than   _____
    c. three baths   _____

16. a. the little creature's feelings   _____
    b. afraid to hurt   _____
    c. she was too   _____

17. a. very simple things here   _____
    b. hear this, Lucy, but we do   _____
    c. you'll be surprised to   _____

18. a. we found a way to punish   _____
    b. the incorrigibles more severely   _____
    c. than the mere repeaters   _____

19. a. they are accepted in our community   _____
    b. when they become   _____
    c. colorless and shapeless again   _____

20. a. that over   _____
    b. we push   _____
    c. the side too   _____

21. a. alone and no longer frightened   _____
    b. her eyes closed,   _____
    c. only Lucy was left,   _____

22. a. she was   _____
    b. when she had opened her eyes   _____
    c. among her family   _____

23. a. to draw them a picture   _____
    b. it would be better   _____
    c. she decided then   _____

C. There are some statements listed below about the narrative. Write **T** for **True** in front of each statement that you think is true. Write **F** for **False** if the statement is not true. Read aloud.

_____ 1. Lucy didn't want to explain.

_____ 2. She was able to understand.

_____ 3. Lucy decided to tell the story.

_____ 4. It was foggy when she climbed the mountain.

_____ 5. Lucy thought of the danger.

_____ 6. She looked forward to her ascent.

_____ 7. At the top she was suddenly surrounded.

_____ 8. The small creatures were smaller than Lucy.

_____ 9. She had been told they existed.

_____ 10. It was too late for her to withdraw.

_____ 11. Lucy was not frightened, but the creatures were.

_____ 12. She smiled and so did the creatures.

_____ 13. The creatures were shapeless and colorless.

_____ 14. One of the creatures spoke to Lucy.

_____ 15. The creature did not speak English.

_____ 16. There were Erutuf people bathing in the lake.

_____ 17. The Erutuf people liked taking a bath.

_____ 18. The bathers were being punished.

_____ 19. They were punished for greed.

_____ 20. Lucy was afraid to hurt the little creature's feelings.

_____ 21. The Erutuf people do simple things.

_____ 22. The incorrigibles were punished more severely than mere repeaters.

_____ 23. The incorrigibles became colorless and shapeless.

_____ 24. The incorrigibles were given good food.

_____ 25. When Lucy cried, the Erutuf people disappeared.

_____ 26. Lucy decided to explain things to her parents.

X. Composition and Discussion

A. In COLUMN I are the beginnings of sentences. In COLUMN II are the completions to sentences of COLUMN I. Select the completion best fitting each sentence in COLUMN I according to the narrative. Read the completed sentences orally. Compose new sentences orally and discuss the narrative.

COLUMN I

1. Lucy was unable to explain
2. As often as she tried
3. There was no one there
4. She became very curious
5. Lucy looked forward to her
6. She was suddenly surrounded
7. They were taller

8. Many bathed
9. She had never seen
10. It was too late
11. Someone had told her

12. Our ancestors had been
13. The Erutuf cried louder
14. Three baths daily are more
15. The simpler
16. Do they love
17. The incorrigibles are given
18. They are banished from
19. There's nothing else
20. I wish to leave
21. When she opened her eyes
22. There was a look of concern

23. She knew that

COLUMN II

a. the top of the mountain.
b. she was with her family.
c. in the clear water.
d. in her parents' faces.
e. color and shape.
f. but Lucy was not afraid.
g. and too excited to think of danger.
h. but they were shapeless.
i. ascent with anticipation.
j. things got too involved.
k. why she had climbed the mountain.
l. such creatures before.
m. for her to withdraw.
n. than she had heard anyone cry.
o. they can eat.
p. this place right now!
q. better to draw a picture.
r. where you come from?
s. she would have to explain.
t. Lucy was unable to e xplain.
u. by a throng of small creatures.
v. that fear is caused by the unknown.
w. its inhabitants before us.

24. As hard as she tried   x. the better.
25. She decided it would be   y. than anyone can stand.

B.   1. Tell us about climbing a mountain.
      2. Describe the small creatures.
      3. Why was Lucy frightened?
      4. How did the Erutuf people punish greed and prejudice?
      5. What do you think of the Erutuf society?

C.   Read the poem aloud. Answer orally the questions listed following the poem.

To Be Different

Why is it that so many who
had wished to be different,
have become so like
one another?
They defy [1] *individuality which*   [1] go against
they had seemingly pursued [2]   [2] striven for
They dress alike, one face
shows less originality [3] *than another.*   [3] creativity
And so in speech and thought
they are but images [4]   [4] mirrors
of each other. The
song they rhythmically [5]   [5] in a pattern, repeated
produce pulsates [6] *mediocrity* [7]   [6] vibrates
no better than the very   [7] inferiority
ways of imitation [8] *they despise!* [9]   [8] copy
And there seems no end to that.   [9] hate

1. What do the words "different" and "individuality" have in common? Discuss in class.
2. Read aloud the lines containing "so." Discuss meaning.
3. Read aloud the lines containing "but." Discuss meaning.
4. Read aloud sentences with the past perfect.
5. Tell about the meaning of this poem.

D. Describe what you see in the picture below.

CHAPTER SEVEN

THE CAVE

IN THIS CHAPTER

Words to remember:

The passive voice
The active voice
The imperative mood – *Let's + infinitive*

Expressions of Location
above-behind-below-between-bottom
downward-far-further-surface-throughout-upward

I. Narrative

A. When summer came, the Campbells were thinking about *vacation*. The children looked forward to the annual family *trip*. Everybody did *except* Mike, for he was *planning* a vacation of his own. His cousin Weldon was coming from Wisconsin for the summer. Mike became *interested* in spelunking when he heard that Weldon had explored caves for over a year. "Don't you forget it," Mrs. Campbell warned Mike. "You must be careful exploring caves." "I'm not a child, Mother." Mike acted hurt. "Even adults get into trouble when they get careless down there," Mrs. Campbell hastened to add. "What Mother's saying is that she *cares* about what happens to you. Do take precautions," Mr. Campbell said. "Sure we will! After all, Weldon is an *experienced* spelunker," Mike assured his parents.

---

vacation: rest from work
trip: journey
except: excluded
planning: arranging
interested: curious
cares: is concerned
experienced: personally tried
bag: sack
reminded: made him remember
leave behind: let remain
lamp: a device for making light
concluded: finished
shown up: returned, came back
shook hands: clasped hands
further: more distant
draft: a current of air
falling: dropping down
downward: to a lower place
passage: narrow way, corridor
columns: pillars
formations: rock origin

demanded: ordered
hit: strike
noise: disagreeable sound
throughout: everywhere
bottom: the lowest place
far: distant
between: in the space that separates two things
ankle: joint between foot and leg
pain: hurt
terrific: intense
grizzly: grey bear
above: at a higher place
gave up: quit
ladder: cord steps
waist: part of body above the hips
upward: to a higher place
crowbar: a long metal bar
surface: exterior
relieved: pleased
safe: secure

B. Weldon arrived on Saturday, as planned. Immediately, the two cousins began their preparations. "Bring a sleeping *bag*," Weldon *reminded* Mike, "like the one I have." He showed his sleeping bag to Mike. "It gets very cold in the hills," Weldon added with a smile. "And don't ever *leave* behind your *lamp*," he *concluded*.

C. The sheriff's deputy in New Braunfels wrote down their names. He also asked the boys to stay at the indicated location. It was assumed that small undiscovered caves could be found in the hills near New Braunfels. "If you haven't *shown up* in three days, the boys'll come up to get you," the sheriff said with a broad grin. "You shouldn't be there alone very long," the deputy said. "Go down slowly, and be careful, boys," he cautioned as they *shook hands* saying goodbye.

D. Below a large limestone bridge, the two explorers saw a hole. They dug *further*. A cave was suddenly discovered by Mike. The boys felt a *draft* of cool air coming through the rock and debris. As they descended, they were hit by small *falling* rocks. "Let's get down lower, Mike! Please hand me the lamp!" Weldon was excited.

E. Further digging revealed a twisting, *downward passage* which opened into a cave. The two explorers crawled through a vast labyrinth of *columns* and crystalline *formations*. "Mike, hand me the rope," Weldon *demanded*. "To get down, you must use the rope," he added, getting ready to descend.

F. Suddenly, Weldon lost his footing. The lamp fell downward. As it *hit* against the walls, the *noise* multiplied *throughout* with an echo. Finally, the lamp hit *bottom* deep below. Weldon did not fall very *far*. His voice came clearly from below as Mike listened anxiously. "My foot is wedged in *between* two rocks. The place is too narrow to free it. I think my left *ankle* is fractured. The *pain is terrific*." It was dark without the lamp, but Weldon felt his way around. "There's a large skeleton down here. It feels like a large animal, maybe a *grizzly*," he called to Mike. "Do be careful down there!" Mike yelled. "I'll go get help!" "Don't worry, Mike. The grizzly's probably been dead for more than eight thousand years." "Don't joke. I'll be back soon."

G. Mike returned half an hour later accompanied by two sheriff's deputies. He was lucky the officers were already searching the hills for them as they'd promised. Weldon was glad to hear voices *above*. "I almost *gave up* on you," he called when he heard the voices of his rescuers. Soon, one of the deputies was lowered on a rope *ladder*. "Always descend carefully," the deputy cautioned. "It was an accident," Mike said. "It could happen to anybody."

H. Everything went fine. A rope was tied round Weldon's *waist*. The deputy above, with Mike's help, pulled Weldon carefully *upward*. Below, the deputy spread the rocks with a *crowbar*, releasing Weldon's ankle. Mike descended to help. Soon, everybody emerged on the *surface*. The deputy examined the injury carefully. "Say, it's not a fracture after all. At the most, it's a sprained ankle." Everyone was *relieved* to be *safe*.

Idea Questions:
1. Why wasn't Mike planning a vacation with his family?
2. How did Mike become interested in spelunking?
3. Did Mrs. Campbell have a good reason to warn Mike?
4. Why is a lamp needed in spelunking?
5. Where did Mike and Weldon go spelunking?
6. When would the sheriff's deputies come to get the boys?
7. What happened to Weldon? How did it happen?
8. Were the two explorers careful?
9. Do you think Weldon was an experienced explorer?
10. What is the MAIN IDEA of this story?

II. Words in Context (Pictographs)

Below are some of the words used in the narrative. Where possible, each word has a [synonym], or it is defined as used in the story. Where possible, an (antonym) is also given. Make up sentences about the pictographs choosing the words you need. Read aloud.

Example : [spelunking] = Mike was interested in spelunking.

A. and B.
look forward to [**anticipate**] *(dread);* annual [**yearly**] ; spelunking [**cave exploring**] ; explore [**investigate**] *(ignore);* cave [**underground chamber**] ; warn [**caution**] *(encourage);* trouble [**difficulty**] *(pleasure);* careless [**reckless**] *(careful);* hasten [**hurry**] *(slow down);* precaution [**care**] *(carelessness)*; assure [**promise**] ; immediately [**at once**] *(later);* preparation [**arrangement**] *(unpreparedness)*

Drawing of paragraph A & B

C., D. and E.
sheriff [**county law enforcement officer**] ; deputy [**representative of law enforcement**] ; indicated [**specified**] *(unspecified);* location [**place**] ; assume [**suppose**] *(know);* discover [**find**] *(search);* broad [**wide**] *(narrow);* bridge [**span**] ; hole [**opening**] ; dig [**excavate**] *(bury);* draft [**current**] ; rock [**large stone**] ; debris [**rubble**] ; reveal [**disclose**] *(hide);* twisting [**curving**] *(straight);* crawl [**creep**] *(run);* vast

Drawing of paragraph C, D & E

[**immense**] *(small);* labyrinth [**maze**] *(straight passage);* crystalline [**clear**] *(unclear);* rope [**cord**] ; footing [**support**] ; multiply [**increased**] *(decrease);* echo [**reverberation**] ; halt [**end**] *(continue);* deep [**profound**] *(shallow)*

F., G. and H.
clearly [**plainly**] *(indistinctly);* wedge [**constrict**] *(release);* narrow [**tight**] *(wide);* fracture [**break**] *(mend);* dark [**obscure**] *(light);* skeleton [**bony framework**]; joke [**josh**] *(be serious);* accompany [**escort**] *(be alone);* lucky [**fortunate**] *(unfortunate);* search [**look for**] *(discover);* rescue [**save**] *(endanger);* lower [**let down**] *(raise);* accident [**mishap**] *(plan);* tie [**secure**] *(untie);* pull [**tow**] *(push);* spread [**separate**] *(converge);* release [**free**] *(confine);* emerge [**come out**] *(go in);* examine [**investigate**] *(answer);* injury [**damage**]; sprained [**twisted**]

Drawing of paragraphs F, G & H

III. Structures [Phrases]

Below are some phrases taken from the narrative. Make complete sentences and read them aloud.

1. about   -vacation
2. forward   -look   -to   -trip
3. interested   -get   -in   -spelunking
4. an   -be   -experienced   -spelunker
5. at   -stay   -the   -location
6. below   -cave   -a   -bridge
7. of   -draft   -cool   -air
8. like   -look   -a large   -animal
9. already   -be   -searching   -hills
10. round   -tie   -Weldon's   -rope   -waist

IV. Sentences

A. Read the following sentences aloud. Repeat, substituting where possible, the synonym of the word in italics, or a phrase that explains the meaning. Make other necessary changes.

Example : Mike *promised* to be careful.
Mike *assured* his mother he would be careful.

1. The children *looked forward* to the trip.
2. You must be careful *exploring caves*.
3. Weldon *warned*.
4. Mike *assured* his parents.
5. Weldon *arrived* on Saturday.
6. They began their *preparations*.
7. The *sheriff* took down their names.
8. Small *caves* could be found in the hills.
9. A cave was *discovered*.
10. They were hit by small *rocks*.
11. They crawled through a *labyrinth*.
12. The foot was *wedged* in between rocks.
13. He saw *clearly* a skeleton down there.
14. It was a *narrow* passage.
15. Weldon *crawled* into the cave.
16. The deputy examined the *fracture*.

B. Fill in the following blanks with words from the narrative. Each space may be filled by a word or phrase. Do not refer back to the narrative. Where possible, use variations of the missing words. Read aloud.

When summer _____, the Campbells _____ about vacation. The children looked _____ to the annual _____ trip. Mike was _____ a vacation of his _____. His cousin Weldon _____ for the _____ from Wisconsin. Mike got _____ in _____.

Weldon _____ on Saturday. The two cousins _____ their _____.
  The sheriff's deputy _____ their names. He_____ the boys to
_____ at the _____ location. It was _____ that small _____ caves
_____ be found in the hills _____ New Braunfels. "You shouldn't be
there _____very _____," the _____ said. "Go _____ slowly, and be
_____, boys."

Below a _____ limestone _____, the two saw a _____. A _____
was suddenly _____ by Mike. The boys _____ a draft of _____ air
coming _____ the rock and _____. As they _____, they were _____
by small rocks.

Further _____ revealed a _____ downward passage which _____ into
a _____.

Suddenly, Weldon _____ his _____. The _____ fell_____. Weldon did
not _____ very _____. It was _____ without the _____, but Weldon
_____ his way_____.

Mike _____ half an hour_____ accompanied by two _____ deputies.
The officers _____ already _____ the hills for them. One of the
deputies was _____ on a ladder. "It was an _____," Mike said.

Everything _____ fine. A rope was _____ round Weldon's _____. Mike
_____ to help. Soon, _____emerged on the _____. The deputy _____
the _____ carefully. Everyone was _____.

V. Grammar (Points of Interest)

A. The Passive Voice

Until now we have used the ACTIVE voice. The doer of the action was
the subject in the ACTIVE VOICE. The one who was acted upon, the
RECEIVER, was the *object*. In the PASSIVE VOICE, the original
RECEIVER becomes the *subject*, and the original *doer* of the action
becomes the object of the preposition *by*.

Active Voice :   Mike *(doer of the action)* discovered a cave *(receiver of the action)*.

Passive Voice :   A cave *(receiver of the action)* was discovered by *Mike (doer of the action)*.

Active Voice :   Small falling rocks *(doers of the action)* hit explorers *(receivers of the action)*.

Passive Voice :   The explorers *(receivers of the action)* were hit by falling rocks *(doers of the action)*.

B. The Imperative Mood

The IMPERATIVE MOOD can be expressed by a *simple verb* form. It expresses *commands, requests, or instructions.*

1.   Singular and plural, second person (the subject *you* is understood):
     Take a train.
     Don't take a train. (negative)
     Bring a sleeping bag.
     Don't bring a sleeping bag. (negative)

2.   First and second person together :
     Let's get down lower.
     Let's not get down lower. (negative)
     Let's see what's down there.
     Let's not see what's down there. (negative)

3.   An adverb of frequency may precede the imperative verb :
     Always descend carefully.
     Don't *ever* leave your lamp behind.

4.   In direct address, a noun may precede the imperative verb, or it may follow it :
     Mike, hand me the rope.
     Hand me the rope, *Mike.*

5. The pronoun *you* is often used, as in the following imperative sentences :
    a. To get down, *you* must use the rope.
        Don't *you* forget it.

    b. *You* must be careful.
        You shouldn't be there alone.
        You will see the light at the other end.

6. To ask earnestly, or to entreat, you use the verb *do*:
        Do be careful down there.
        Do take precautions.

7. Words of politeness sometimes precede or follow the imperative verb in a request.
        Please, hand me the lamp.

    Will
    Would you (please) remember the light?

    Go down slowly, *please*.

    Remember to come next summer, *please*.

    Stop the noise, *will* *would* *you (please)*?

8. Some commands appear as printed signs or slogans :

NO SMOKING	KEEP OFF THE GRASS
DO NOT ENTER	KEEP OUT
RIGHT TURN ONLY	NO PARKING

VI. Word Recognition

A. Circle the word (phrase) in Column II most like the word in Column I, and circle the word (phrase) in Column III most unlike the word in Column I. This oral identification of words ought to be timed.

COLUMN I	COLUMN II	COLUMN III
1. **accompany**	a. escort b. help c. carry	a. lack b. hinder c. leave
2. **assume**	a. possess b. suppose c. carry	a. know b. hinder c. sell
3. **broad**	a. warm b. wide c. hot	a. far b. narrow c. unsafe
4. **careless**	a. sudden b. abrupt c. reckless	a. careful b. usual c. married
5. **crawl**	a. carry b. creep c. relax	a. run b. work c. hinder
6. **dark**	a. indicative b. obscure c. undecided	a. plain b. light c. narrow
7. **deep**	a. big b. profound c. vague	a. creeping b. excavated c. shallow
8. **dig**	a. argue b. expose c. excavate	a. bury b. ignore c. assume
9. **discover**	a. find b. locate c. place	a. assume b. suppose c. search

10. **explore**
   a. investigate
   b. sell
   c. cross

   a. behave
   b. ignore
   c. work

11. **hasten**
   a. overturn
   b. quicken
   c. tip over

   a. slow down
   b. control
   c. regulate

12. **immediately**
   a. so on
   b. at once
   c. haltingly

   a. after a while
   b. specifically
   c. lacking

13. **indicated**
   a. halted
   b. dragged
   c. specified

   a. concealed
   b. sold
   c. unspecified

14. **look forward to**
   a. go down
   b. anticipate
   c. stop

   a. hinder
   b. purchase
   c. dread

15. **multiply**
   a. suppose
   b. argue
   c. increase

   a. decrease
   b. discover
   c. expose

16. **narrow**
   a. small
   b. tight
   c. large

   a. wide
   b. straight
   c. vast

17. **precaution**
   a. care
   b. profession
   c. task

   a. disorder
   b. worry
   c. carelessness

B. Pick the right expression. Complete the following sentences with the term that best fits the situation. Read aloud.

assure	release	reveals
twisting	spread	trouble
deep	warm	vacation
location	accompany	discover
accident	crawl	crystalline

1. If you have a mishap, we assume that you had an _____.
2. In places that are very narrow you can only _____.
3. When you have worked hard all year, you deserve a _____.
4. If you escort someone, you can also say that you _____ her.
5. When you search for something, you may _____ it.
6. When you promise something, you _____ someone.
7. On a cold night it is good to keep _____.
8. Another way to say curving is _____.
9. When you face difficulties you're in _____.
10. If nature discloses something, it _____ it.

C. In the space on the left write the word(s) that would best fit the expression in bold print. Make other necessary changes. Read aloud.

_____ 1. The children **anticipated** the annual trip.
_____ 2. Mike got interested in **cave exploring**.
_____ 3. Weldon is an **experienced** spelunker.
_____ 4. They began their preparations **at once**.
_____ 5. Stay at the **indicated** place.
_____ 6. It was **assumed** there were caves.
_____ 7. The deputy had a **wide** grin.
_____ 8. There was a large bedrock **bridge**.
_____ 9. The boys **excavated** further.
_____ 10. They felt a cool **current of air**.
_____ 11. It came through the **rubble**.
_____ 12. There was a **curving** passage.
_____ 13. The explorers **crept** through the passage.
_____ 14. Mike handed Weldon the **cord**.

_____ 15. The noise reproduced itself with an **echo.**
_____ 16. The flashlight **ended** its fall below.
_____ 17. Weldon's voice came from below **plainly.**
_____ 18. His foot was **wedged** between two rocks.
_____ 19. He thought his ankle was **broken.**
_____ 20. Don't **josh**, Mike, go get help!
_____ 21. Mike returned **escorted** by two deputies.
_____ 22. The deputy was   on a rope ladder.
_____ 23. A rope was **secured** round his waist.
_____ 24. They **towed** him upward.
_____ 25. The deputy **freed** his foot.
_____ 26. Everybody **came out** on the surface.

VII. Concept Recognition

Fill in the most appropriate word (phrase) to express the CONCEPT of sentence according to the narrative. Read the complete sentence aloud.

A. The Campbell children looked forward to _____.
   1. the annual trip   3. thinking
   2. the planning   4. the summer

B. When they get careless, even adults _____.
   1. investigate   3. get in trouble
   2. explore   4. ignore

C. Mike assured his parents that he would_____.
   1. anticipate the trip   3. find a cave
   2. be careful   4. be careless

D. When Weldon arrived, the two cousins began their_____.
   1. preparations   3. exploration
   2. trip   4. pleasure

E. They took sleeping bags because_____.
   1. Mrs. Campbell cautioned 3. they took a lamp
   2. it gets cold in the hills 4. they were experienced

F. If they haven't shown up in three days, the deputies would_____.
1. come up to get them
2. take precautions
3. be surprised
4. plan a trip

G. When they felt a current of cool air coming through the rock, they found_____.
1. a bear
2. a passage
3. a bridge
4. a way back

H. Weldon demanded a rope because he wanted_____.
1. to get down
2. to climb
3. to get ready
4. to explore

I. The flashlight fell when Weldon_____.
1. tied the rope
2. lost his footing
3. looked up
4. talked

J. Weldon was unable to move because_____.
1. he fell very far
2. he yelled loud
3. his foot was wedged between rocks
4. his ankle was fractured

K. A rope was tied round Weldon's waist to_____.
1. pull him up
2. secure his descent
3. keep him in place
4. help him explore

L. The deputy spread the rocks to_____.
1. explore them
2. release Weldon's foot
3. examine them
4. lower Mike

VIII. Telling the Meaning

A. Place a check mark (✔) in front of the word in COLUMN II that best fits the MEANING of the word in COLUMN I. Read aloud a complete sentence using this word.

COLUMN I	COLUMN II

1. accident
   - _____ a. search
   - _____ b. mishap
   - _____ c. plan

2. anticipate
   - _____ a. look forward to
   - _____ b. dread
   - _____ c. explore

3. arrangement
   - _____ a. preparation
   - _____ b. chance
   - _____ c. unpreparedness

4. profound
   - _____ a. deep
   - _____ b. modest
   - _____ c. shallow

5. care
   - _____ a. design
   - _____ b. carelessness
   - _____ c. precaution

6. caution
   - _____ a. encourage
   - _____ b. warn
   - _____ c. explore

7. creep
   - _____ a. crawl
   - _____ b. run
   - _____ c. gain

8. curving
   - _____ a. uneven terrain
   - _____ b. straight
   - _____ c. twisting

9. difficulty
   - _____ a. order
   - _____ b. pleasure
   - _____ c. trouble

10. disclose
    _____ a. hide
    _____ b. discover
    _____ c. reveal

11. escort
    _____ a. be alone
    _____ b. accompany
    _____ c. relax

12. excavate
    _____ a. dig
    _____ b. bury
    _____ c. compensate

13. fracture
    _____ a. shout
    _____ b. mend
    _____ c. break

14. halt
    _____ a. close
    _____ b. continue
    _____ c. end

15. investigate
    _____ a. ignore
    _____ b. warn
    _____ c. explore

B. Recognize words in the Narrative.

1. Which word in paragraph A. means "rest from work"? _____
2. Which word in paragraph A. means "is concerned"? _____
3. Which word in paragraph B. means "made him remember"? _____
4. Which word in paragraph B. means "a device for making light"? _____
5. Which word in paragraph C. means "specified"? _____
6. Which word in paragraph C. means "returned"? _____
7. Which word in paragraph C. means "clasped hands"? _____
8. Which word in paragraph D. means "more distant"? _____
9. Which word in paragraph D. means "a current of air"? _____
10. Which word in paragraph D. means "dropping down"? _____
11. Which word in paragraph E. means "rock origin"? _____

12. Which word in paragraph F. means "disagreeable sound"? _____
13. Which word in paragraph F. means "the lowest place"? _____
14. Which word in paragraph G. means "let down"? _____
15. Which word in paragraph G. means "cord steps"? _____
16. Which word in paragraph H. means "a long metal bar"? _____

C. Return to Exercise A. Place two check marks (✔✔) in front of the word in COLUMN II that is the ANTONYM of the word in COLUMN I. Read aloud a complete sentence using this word.

D. Select one of the three (3) words (phrases) that best fulfills the MEANING of the sentence according to the narrative. Insert the word in the blank space. Read the completed sentence aloud

1. The Campbells were thinking about vacation because _____.
   a. summer came   b. they liked   c. they planned exploring

2. Mike didn't look forward to a family trip because he_____.
   a. was unhappy   b. didn't like   c. planned a vacation
                                                   of his own

3. Mrs. Campbell cautioned Mike because she _____.
   a. was happy   b. cared   c. took precautions

4. Mike got interested in spelunking when _____.
   a. he heard   b. he heard that   c. he heard
      about the   that Weldon   about hills
      precautions   explored caves

5. Mike was sure they would take precautions because _____.
   a. Weldon was   b. the deputy   c. Weldon was an
      coming   was there   experienced spelunker

6. The deputies would come up to get the boys _____.
   a. after three days   b. when they   c. discovered the cave
                            asked for help

7. A cave was discovered by Mike when _____.
   a. they fell inside   b. the boys felt a   c. the rocks hit them
                             draft of cool air

8. Weldon demanded the rope. He wanted to _____.
   a. descend   b. climb   c. crawl

9. There was a loud noise when the lamp _____.
   a. came to a halt   b. hit the walls   c. stopped falling

10. Weldon was unable to ascend because _____.
    a. he had no lamp   b. he was unhappy   c. his foot was wedged in
                                                  between two rocks

11. Mike was lucky because the officers were _____.
    a. in New Braunfels   b. already searching c. came to the cave
                             the hills

12. To get Weldon out, they had to _____.
    a. tie a rope   b. search the hills   c. lower the ladder
       round his waist   for him

13. To get Weldon's foot free, the deputy _____.
    a. spread the rope   b. spread the rocks   c. pulled him up

14. Everybody emerged happy because _____.
    a. Weldon's ankle   b. they saw   c. Mike was a spelunker
       was only sprained   the grizzly

IX. Comprehension [Exercises]

A. Place a check mark (✔) in front of the correct response to each of the statements according to the narrative.

1. The Campbells looked forward to
   _____ a. the annual family trip.
   _____ b. spelunking.
   _____ c. Weldon's visit.

2. Mike was planning
   _____ a. a trip with the family.
   _____ b. a vacation of his own.
   _____ c. a trip to Wisconsin.

3. Mrs. Campbell warned Mike about
   _____ a. going on vacation.
   _____ b. exploring caves.
   _____ c. his cousin Weldon.

4. Mike acted hurt because
   _____ a. Mrs. Campbell cared.
   _____ b. Mrs. Campbell warned him.
   _____ c. Weldon didn't arrive.

5. When did Weldon arrive?
   _____ a. on Sunday.
   _____ b. on Saturday.
   _____ c. on Monday.

6. Why did Weldon bring a sleeping bag?
   _____ a. because it gets cold in the hills.
   _____ b. because the cave is deep.
   _____ c. because he wanted to sleep.

7. The deputies would come up to get the boys
   _____ a. if they called the sheriff.
   _____ b. if they got lost.
   _____ c. if they didn't show up in three days.

8. What was discovered by Mike?
   _____ a. a cave.
   _____ b. a draft.
   _____ c. a rock.

9. What hit the boys as they descended?
      _____ a. the draft.
      _____ b. the small falling rocks.
      _____ c. the lamp.

10. To get down lower, Weldon needed
      _____ a. a lamp and a rope.
      _____ b. a ladder.
      _____ c. a sleeping bag.

11. Weldon could not come up because
      _____ a. he found a cave.
      _____ b. his foot was wedged in between rocks.
      _____ c. he had no ladder.

12. What did Weldon find in the cave?
      _____ a. a man.
      _____ b. a lamp.
      _____ c. a skeleton.

13. Why was Weldon glad?
      _____ a. he heard a grizzly.
      _____ b. lie heard voices.
      _____ c. lie saw the deputies.

14. To get Weldon up, they
      _____ a. tied a rope round his waist.
      _____ b. gave him a rope.
      _____ c. gave him a lamp.

15. To release Weldon's foot, the deputy
      _____ a. pulled.
      _____ b. spread the rocks.
      _____ c. pushed.

16. What did the deputy say?
     _____ a. Weldon's foot was fractured.
     _____ b. Weldon's lamp was broken.
     _____ c. Weldon's ankle was sprained.

B. Below there are three (3) different thoughts expressed in each of the exercises. Assign the proper sequence (order of THOUGHT) according to the narrative, by numbering 1 to 3. Read aloud.

1. a. the Campbells were thinking   _____
    b. when summer came   _____
    c. about vacation   _____

2. a. the annual family trip   _____
    b. looked forward to   _____
    c. the children   _____

3. a. get into trouble   _____
    b. even adults   _____
    c. when they get careless   _____

4. a. as planned   _____
    b. on Saturday   _____
    c. Weldon arrived   _____

5. a. took down their names   _____
    b. the sheriff's deputy   _____
    c. in New Braunfels   _____

6. a. to stay   _____
    b. at the indicated location   _____
    c. he also asked the boys   _____

7. a. it was assumed that small _____
    b. be found in the hills   _____
    c. undiscovered caves could   _____

8. a. the two explorers saw a hole _____
   b. below a large _____
   c. limestone bridge _____

9. a. by small falling rocks _____
   b. they were hit _____
   c. as they descended, _____

10. a. further digging revealed _____
   b. which opened into a cave _____
   c. a twisting, downward passage _____

11. a. use the rope _____
   b. you must _____
   c. to get down _____

12. a. throughout with an echo _____
   b. as it hit against the walls, _____
   c. the noise multiplied _____

13. a. somewhere deep below _____
   b. hit bottom _____
   c. finally, the lamp _____

14. a. as Mike listened anxiously _____
   b. his voice came _____
   c. clearly from below _____

15. a. the lamp, but Weldon _____
   b. felt his way around him _____
   c. it was dark without _____

16. a. accompanied by sheriff's deputies _____
   b. half an hour later _____
   c. Mike returned _____

17. a. he was lucky the officers   _____

     b. for them as they promised   _____

     c. were already searching the hills   _____

18. a. Weldon was glad   _____

     b. voices above   _____

     c. to hear   _____

19. a. with Mike's help, pulled   _____

     b. Weldon carefully upward   _____

     c. the deputy above,   _____

20. a. releasing Weldon's ankle   _____

     b. the rocks with a crowbar,   _____

     c. below, the deputy spread   _____

21. a. examined   _____

     b. the deputy   _____

     c. the injury carefully   _____

C. There are some statements listed below about the narrative. Write T for True in front of each statement if you think it is true. Write F for False if the statement is not true. Read aloud.

_____ 1. The children looked forward to the family trip.

_____ 2. Mike looked forward to the family trip.

_____ 3. Weldon was a spelunker.

_____ 4. Mrs. Campbell warned Mike.

_____ 5. Mike didn't act hurt.

_____ 6. Weldon arrived on Monday.

_____ 7. It gets cold in the hills.

_____ 8. To explore caves you must have a lamp.

_____ 9. The deputy wrote down their names.

_____ 10. There were caves in the hills.

_____ 11. There was a hole below a limestone bridge.

_____ 12. A cave was discovered by Weldon

_____ 13. A draft of cool air came through the rocks.

_____ 14. The boys were hit by small rocks.

_____ 15. Weldon was excited.

_____ 16. A passage opened into a cave.

_____ 17. Suddenly, Mike lost his footing.

_____ 18. The lamp fell downward.

_____ 19. The falling lamp made a noise.

_____ 20. Weldon fell very far.

_____ 21. In the cave he found a skeleton.

_____ 22. The skeleton was that of a man.

_____ 23. An accident can happen to anybody.

_____ 24. Everyone was happy.

_____ 25. The deputy pulled Weldon upward.

_____ 26. Weldon's ankle was fractured.

X. Composition and Discussion

A. In Column I are beginnings of sentences. In column II are the completions to the sentences of Column I. Select the completion best fitting each sentence in Column I according to the narrative. Read the completed sentences orally. Compose new sentences orally and discuss the narrative.

COLUMN I	COLUMN II
1. The children looked forward	a. his parents.
2. His cousin Weldon	b. as planned.
3. Even the adults get into trouble	c. crawled through a labyrinth.
4. Mike assured	d. without the lamp.
5. Weldon arrived on Saturday	e. somewhere deep below.
6. Below a large bridge	f. very far.
7. A cave was suddenly	g. already searching the hills.
8. The two explorers	h. was lowered on a rope ladder.
9. The lamp hit bottom	i. when they get careless.
10. Weldon did not fall	j. the two explorers saw a hole.
11. It was dark	k. half an hour later.
12. Mike returned	l. discovered by Mike.
13. The officers were	m. emerged on the surface.

14. One of the deputies   n.   to the annual family trip.
15. Soon, everybody   o.   was coming from Wisconsin.

B. 1.   Describe a cave.
    2.   What do you need for exploring caves?
    3.   Tell us about Mike's and Weldon's trip.
    4.   Tell us about the rescue.

C. Read this poem aloud. Answer orally the questions listed following the poem

They say. . .

He speaks, and it is done.
He makes things grow up high
into the sky, and down   [1] surface
deep into the ground [1] *. . .*

He says, "Let there be light!"
And it is light. And darkness
follows, for both
are part of life . . .
Yet too much rain   [2] destroy
will ravage [2] *in a flood, while*   [3] dry
the burning sun can   [4] fruitful
parch [3] *this fertile* [4] *earth . .*   [5] cannot see
They say that man is blinded [5]   [6] too much
by excessive [6] *light, and only*   [7] shadow
the shade [7] *brings him*   [8] needed
the longed for [8] *rest . . .*

1.   Identify the *imperative* in this poem.
2.   Identify the *passive* in this poem.
3.   Discuss the meaning of the second verse.
4.   What is the meaning of the words "light" and "darkness"?
5.   What does the poem tell you? Discuss it in class.

D. Describe what you see in the picture below.

SAVING FACE

I. Narrative

A. His family was happy when Professor Stuart signed with the *community college*. The professor had been *looking for* a *job* since January. He was glad when he was *offered* the position of *Chairman* of the English *Department*.

B. Now, the Stuarts went out to shop for a house. There was Professor John Stuart, his wife, Lilian, and their two sons, Shawn and Kip. Mrs. Stuart was of Chinese descent. John Stuart *married* Lilian while they were students at M.Y.U. It was the second year of college for him. John had been learning Chinese as a minor *subject*. Lilian was a student from China. Knowing Lilian improved John's *knowl-*

---

community college: two-year college
looking for: searching
job: work
offered: presented, given
chairman: director, head
department: section
married: wed, husband and wife
subject: task, discipline
knowledge: understanding ways
sold: traded
larger: bigger
expensive: costly
besides: anyway
meeting: getting together
gatherings: meetings
immediately: right away
moved (into): changed place of dwelling
chore: job
joined: got together (with)
helping: assisting, aiding

working: laboring
overheard: heard secretly
stay out: live some where else
unaccustomed: not used to
citizenship: became citizen
residence: living in one place
swearing-in: oath taking
ceremony: formal act, ritual
proud: joyful
sponsored: was responsible (for)
celebrate: honor, observe festivities
fell (on): came out (on)
unfriendly: hostile, unkind
judgment: decision
throughout: during the whole (night)
success: (had) good result
missed: regretted the absence (of)
away: gone
until: till, up to the time (when)
in vain: fruitless, without value
blushed: became red in the face
second thought: after thought

edge of that difficult language. Some thought he had been speaking Chinese all his life because it was as good as Lilian's. But John knew he didn't speak as well as his wife. He was always trying hard to improve his knowledge of the language.

C. Not far down the street from the Campbells a house was being *sold*. It was *larger* than the Stuarts needed. It was a big house and more *expensive* than they were able to afford. But John and Lilian liked the neighborhood. *Besides*, the professor had been *meeting* Mr. Campbell at social *gatherings*. They established a friendship *immediately* because Mr. Campbell had also studied at M.Y.U.

D. The Stuarts *moved into* their new home on a Sunday. Moving is always a great *chore*. Some of the neighbors *joined* the Campbells in *helping* the Stuarts with their moving. They had been *working* hard when the Stuarts' next-door neighbor was *overheard* saying: "Why don't these foreigners *stay out* of our neighborhood?" No one answered. The Campbells were worried about the Stuarts who had been *unaccustomed* to prejudice. The neighbor said that the Stuarts might not live in the neighborhood for very long.

E. The second month had gone by. Lilian Stuart received her U.S. citizenship on the twentieth of May. She had been living in the United States for five years by then. That's the required time for residence in the United States before an alien can become a citizen. The swearing-in ceremony was impressive. Mrs. Campbell cried, and Mr. Campbell was proud to have sponsored Lilian.

F. The Stuarts planned a big neighborhood party to celebrate Lilian's citizenship. Her birthday fell on the twenty-fifth of May. They had been waiting for a proper occasion to celebrate. The only problem was Mrs. Fox, the unfriendly neighbor.

G. Lilian learned that the Foxes were going to be away on the twenty-seventh of May. "That's the night I'll give the party," she told John. Her husband didn't always understand Lilian's ways, but he loved her, and he trusted her judgment.

H. The neighbors had been celebrating Lilian's new citizenship throughout the night. The party was a great success. Everyone was happy to welcome the new American. No one missed the Foxes. Only John saw a mysterious twinkle in Lilian's eyes.

I. On the following day Mrs. Fox dropped in at the Stuarts' home. "I must apologize for missing your party, Lilian," she called Mrs. Stuart by her first name. "I am happy you have come to tell me this, Gertrude," Lilian responded. "But... I don't understand..." Gertrude stammered. "Well, it's like this," Lilian went on. "When I found out you were going to be away, I decided to give a party. I planned this to give you a chance not to come. But I had hoped you'd come to apologize, as you did. If you hadn't done this, I'd have given you another chance, and another one after that, until you would understand. I'm glad you came; if not my party would have been in vain."

J. Mrs. Fox suddenly understood. "So this is what they call saving face? How wonderful of you, Lilian, to give me this chance!" she exclaimed. "To do a thing like this you must really care for people! I would come, if you gave me another chance." Gertrude blushed, embarrassed. She embraced the new American heartily. They were going to be friends now. "On second thought," Lilian said with a broad smile, "I wouldn't have missed this for anything."

Idea Questions:

1. Why did Professor Stuart sign with the community college?

2. Was it important for Professor Stuart to improve his knowledge of Chinese?

3. How did Mr. Campbell and Professor Stuart become friends?

4. Why were some neighbors helping the Stuarts?

5. Why were some neighbors unkind to the Stuarts?

6. Was it important to celebrate Lilian's citizenship?

7. Why did Lilian plan her party when the Foxes were absent?

8. Was it nice for Mrs. Fox to apologize?

9. Why did Gertrude become Lilian's friend?

10. What is the MAIN IDEA of this story?

II. Words in Context [Pictographs]

Below are some of the words used in the narrative. Where possible, each word has a [synonym], or it is defined as used in the story. Where possible, an (antonym) is also given. Make up sentences about the pictographs choosing the words you need. Read aloud.

Example: [improve] = The Stuarts bettered their position.

A, B, C, and D.

sign [contract]; position [post]; shop for [select] (sell); descent [origin]; minor [secondary] (major); improve [better] (worsen); sell [trade for money] (buy); afford [have the money for]; establish [secure] (break up)

E, F, G and H.

required [necessary] (unnecessary); residence [habitation]; alien [immigrant] (citizen); ceremony [ritual]; impressive [imposing] (unimpressive); sponsor [support]; celebrate [observe festivities joyfully]; proper [appropriate] (improper); occasion [opportunity]; problem [difficulty] (solution); trust [have faith] (mistrust)

I and J.

following [next] (previous); drop in [visit] (depart); apologize [express regret] (blame); stammer [stutter]; decide [resolve] (hesitate); save [redeem] (lose); embarrass [perplex] (relieve); embrace [hug] (recoil); heartily [sincerely] (insincerely)

Drawing of paragraphs A, B, C & D

III. Structures [Phrases]

Below are some PHRASES taken from the narrative. Make complete sentences and read them aloud.

1. looking	- Stuart	- for	- a job
2. out	- house	- to	- shop
3. of	- Lilian	- Chinese	- descent
4. to	- try	- improve	- his knowledge
5. a	- be	- big	- house
6. at	- be	- social	- gatherings
7. their	- like	- new	- home
8. a	- moving	- great	- chore
9. the	- problem	- unfriendly	- neighbor

Drawing of paragraph E, F, G & H

IV. Sentences

A. Read the following sentences aloud. Repeat, substituting where possible, the synonym of the word in *italics*.

Example : His family liked the *new position*.
His family was happy when he had gotten the *new post*.

1. Professor Stuart *signed* with the community college.

2. The professor had been *shopping* for a job.

3. He was offered a *position*.

4. The Stuarts went to *select* a house.

Drawing of paragraphs I & J

5. John had been *improving* his knowledge of Chinese.

6. John was *trying* to improve his knowledge.

7. A house was being *sold.*

8. It was larger than the one they *required.*

9. They could *afford* the neighborhood.

10. They *established* a friendship.

11. The Stuarts moved into their new *residence.*

12. Moving is always a great *chore.*

13. The Stuarts had been unaccustomed to *prejudice.*

14. They *planned* a neighborhood party.

15. They had been waiting to *celebrate* her citizenship.

16. The only *problem* was Mrs. Fox.

17. He *trusted* her judgment.

18. Everyone *dropped* in to celebrate.

19. John saw a *mysterious* twinkle in her eyes.

20. Mrs. Fox *appeared* at the Stuarts' home.

21. Mrs. Fox suddenly *understood*.

B. Fill in the blanks with words from the narrative. Each space may be filled by a word or phrase. Do not refer back to the narrative. Where possible, use variations of the missing words. Read aloud.

The _____ was_____. Professor Stuart_____ with the community college. The professor had _____ for a _____. He was a _____.

The Stuarts went out to _____ for a _____. John Stuart _____ Lilian at M.Y.U. It was the _____ year of _____ for _____. John had been _____ Chinese. Lilian was a _____ from China. John was _____ to _____ his knowledge.

A _____ was being _____. It was _____ than what they _____. It was a _____ house. They _____the _____. They _____ a _____.
    The Stuarts _____ into their _____ home. Moving is _____ a great _____. The Stuarts had been_____ to _____.

The _____ month had gone by. Lilian _____ her U.S. _____. She had been _____ in the United States for five _____ by _____. That's the _____ time for _____ in the United States before an _____ can _____ a citizen.

They _____ a _____ party. They had been _____ to _____. The only _____ was Mrs. Fox, the _____ neighbor.

The Foxes were going to be _____. "I'll give a _____ that _____." Her _____ didn't _____ understand her. But the _____ her _____, and he _____ her _____.

The _____ had been _____ Lilian's new _____ throughout the night. The _____ was great _____. Everyone was _____ to _____ the new _____.

Mrs. Fox _____ at the Stuarts' _____. "I'm _____ you came; if not my _____ would have been in _____," Lilian said.

Mrs. Fox _____ understood. She _____ the new American. They were gong to be _____ now. "I wouldn't have _____ this for _____," Lilian said.

V. Grammar (Points of Interest)

A. The **Past Perfect Continuous** tells about an action or a condition that takes place *up to a certain time* in the past. We use the forms : *had + been + verb + ing*

The professor *had been looking* for a job.

John *had been learning* Chinese.

Some thought he *had been speaking* Chinese all his life.

The professor *had been meeting* Mr. Campbell at social gatherings.

They *had been waiting* for a proper occasion to celebrate.

The neighbors *had been celebrating* Lilian's citizenship throughout the night.

B. The **Sequence of Tenses** occurs most often in Noun Clauses.

If the MAIN VERB is in the PAST TENSE, it is often accompanied by a PAST VERB in the dependent clause.

A MAIN VERB in any other tense does not require a special verb form in the dependent clause.

MAIN VERB	in the PRESENT	in the PAST
Adverbial Clause	The Stuarts *are staying* here because they *are* my friends.	The man *stayed* here because he *was* ill.
Adjective Clause	The Campbells *are worried* about the Stuarts who *have been unaccustomed* to prejudice.	The Campbells *were worried* about the Stuarts who *had been unaccustomed* to prejudice.
Noun Clause	The neighbor *says* that the Stuarts *may not live* in this neighbor-hood for very long.	The neighbor *said* that the Stuarts *might not live* in this neighbor-hood for very long.

C. More uses of *the.*

1. **The** is frequently used with **ordinal numbers**:
   It was *the second* year of college for him.
   The second month had gone by.
   Lilian Stuart received her U.S. citizenship on *the twentieth* of May.
   Her birthday fell on *the twenty-fifth* of May.
   The Foxes were gong to be away on *the twenty-seventh* of May.

2. **The** can also be used with **adjectives** in a time or space sequence:
   On the following day Mrs. Fox appeared at the Stuarts' home.

D. *Would* is used in **conditional** clauses.

   "*If* you hadn't done this, *I would* have given you another chance."
   "I'm glad you came; *if* not, my party *would* have been in vain."
   "I *would* come *if* you gave me another chance."

VI. Word Recognition

A. Circle the word(s) in Column II most like the word in Column I, and circle the word(s) in Column III most unlike the word in Column I. This oral identification of words ought to be timed.

COLUMN I	COLUMN II	COLUMN III
1. **afford**	a. have the money for b. practice c. listen	a. need b. misbehave c. retain
2. **apologize**	a. declare b. express regret c. testify	a. repress b. be wrong c. blame
3. **decide**	a. resolve b. testify c. confirm	a. precede b. hesitate c. avoid
4. **embarrass**	a. dominate b. perplex c. separate	a. relieve b. advise c. counsel
5. **establish**	a. control b. secure c. detain	a. let go b. tip over c. break up
6. **following**	a. beyond b. next c. farther	a. previous b. near c. orderly
7. **heartily**	a. sincerely b. sympathetically c. kindly	a. courtly b. unkind c. insincerely

8. **impressive**

    a. wealthy
    b. imposing
    c. protected

    a. unimpressive
    b. unsafe
    c. usual

9. **improve**

    a. rest
    b. better
    c. listen

    a. hinder
    b. worsen
    c. lack

10. **minor**

    a. secondary
    b. happy
    c. grumpy

    a. at rest
    b. major
    c. active

B. Pick the right expression. Complete the following sentences with the term that best fits the situation. Read aloud.

problem	proper	save
sell	shop for	trust
position	required	impressive
celebrated	following	decided
save	embarrassed	embrace

1. If you have difficulties, you can say that you have a_____.

2. When a person is perplexed, it is the same as being_____.

3. Something that is necessary is_____.

4. Having faith in something means having_____.

5. If a ceremony is imposing, you can say that it is _____.

6. Certain things have to be resolved or _____.

7. A person's birthday is _____ once a year.

8. When you receive a post, you can say that you got a _____.

9. When planning a party, you have to _____ many things.

10. Something that is appropriate is _____.

C. In the space on the left write the word(s) that best fit the expression in **bold print**. Make other necessary changes. Read aloud.

1. The professor was offered a **position**.

2. The Stuarts went out to **select** a house.

3. Lilian was of Chinese **origin**.

4. John's **secondary subject** was Chinese.

5. They **secured** a friendship.

6. Five years of **habitation** are **necessary**.

7. An **alien** became a citizen.

8. The **formality** of swearing-in was impressive.

9. Mr. Campbell **supported** Lilian's citizenship.

10. The neighbors **observed** Lilian's citizenship.

11. It was the **proper opportunity**.

12. John **had faith** in Lilian's judgment.

13. On the next day, Mrs. Fox **dropped in**.

14. She came to **excuse** herself.

15. Mrs. Fox **stuttered**.

16. Lilian **decided** to have a party.

17. Mrs. Fox **hugged** Lilian **heartily**.

VII. Concept Recognition

Fill in the word (phrase) most fitting to express the concept of the sentence according to the narrative. Read the complete sentence aloud.

A. The Stuart family was happy when the professor _____.
    1. got a position   3. learned Chinese
    2. met the Campbells   4. looked for a job

B. John Stuart knew his knowledge of Chinese was _____.
1. as good as Lilian's
2. not as good as Lilian's
3. better than Lilian's
4. as good as it could be

C. He worked hard to _____.
1. improve his friendship
2. be a good chairman
3. improve his knowledge of the language.
4. learn more about Lilian

D. They bought a bigger house than they needed because _____.
1. the Foxes lived there.
2. they liked the neighborhood
3. they met at social gatherings
4. Lilian liked to give parties

E. Some neighbors helped the Stuarts with their moving because _____.
1. they liked the Campbells
2. they liked the neighborhood
3. moving is a great chore
4. they studied at M.Y.U.

F. With her remark, Mrs. Fox showed _____.
1. her prejudice
2. her friendship
3. her worry
4. her happiness

G. The Campbells were worried because the Stuarts might be _____.
1. hurt by the prejudice
2. afraid
3. accustomed to prejudice
4. prejudiced like Mrs. Fox

H. Lilian waited five years in residence to receive her citizenship because _____.
1. she was in China
2. she studied at M.Y.U.
3. she liked the United States
4. it is the required time

I. Mrs. Campbell cried at the ceremony because it _____.
1. took a long time
2. was required
3. was impressive
4. was the twentieth of May

J. The Stuarts planned a big party to _____
    1. celebrate Lilian's citizenship   3. invite unfriendly neighbors
    2. invite Mrs. Fox   4. have fun

K. Lilian planned the party when_____.
    1. it was her birthday   3. John was at the college
    2. the Foxes were away   4. Kip and Shawn were at school

L. John didn't always understand Lilian, but he _____.
    1. listened to her   3. had faith in her
    2. had faith in himself   4. had faith in his judgment

M. Mrs. Fox appeared at the Stuarts' home to_____.
    1. come to the party   3. be prejudiced
    2. apologize for   4. speak to John
       missing the party

N. Lilian was happy because she knew that_____.
    1. her party was not in vain   3. she gave a good party
    2. Mrs. Fox was prejudiced   4. John was happy

O. Mrs. Fox called Lilian by her first name to show_____.
    1. prejudice   3. worry
    2. friendship   4. happiness

P. Lilian gave Mrs. Fox a chance to_____.
    1. worry   3. be away
    2. be happy   4. save face

Q. Mrs. Fox realized that Lilian _____.
    1. really cared for people   3. loved John
    2. was from China   4. gave good parties

VIII. Telling the Meaning

A. Place a check mark (✔) in front of the word in COLUMN II that best fits the MEANING of the word in COLUMN I. Read aloud a complete sentence using this word.

COLUMN I   COLUMN II

1. **appropriate**
   _____ a. grumpy
   _____ b. proper
   _____ c. improper

2. **better**
   _____ a. improve
   _____ b. worsen
   _____ c. learn

3. **difficulty**
   _____ a. problem
   _____ b. task
   _____ c. solution

4. **embrace**
   _____ a. recoil
   _____ b. hug
   _____ c. possess

5. **express regret**
   _____ a. blame
   _____ b. apologize
   _____ c. resolve

6. **have faith**
   _____ a. hold on
   _____ b. trust
   _____ c. mistrust

7. **imposing**
   _____ a. unimpressive
   _____ b. impressive
   _____ c. unafraid

8. **next**

_____ a. previous
_____ b. following
_____ c. modest

9. **offer**

_____ a. present
_____ b. say
_____ c. withhold

10. **perplex**

_____ a. relieve
_____ b. relax
_____ c. confuse

11. **redeem**

_____ a. save
_____ b. share
_____ c. lose

B. Recognize words in the Narrative.

1. Which word in paragraph A. means "two year college"? _____

2. Which word in paragraph A. means "presented"? _____

3. Which word in paragraph B. means "husband and wife"?
_____

4. Which word in paragraph B. means "understanding"? _____

5. Which word in paragraph C. means "have the money"? _____

6. Which word in paragraph C. means "secure"? _____

7. Which word in paragraph C. means "getting together"? _____

8. Which word in paragraph D. means "changed place of dwelling"?
_____

9. Which word in paragraph E. means "immigrant"? _____

10. Which word in paragraph F. means "opportunity"? _____

11. Which word in paragraph F. means "become citizen"? _____

12. Which word in paragraph G. means "decision"? _____

13. Which word in paragraph H. means "during the whole night"?

_____

14. Which word in paragraph H. means "regretted the absence"?

_____

15. Which word in paragraph I. means "without value"? _____

16. Which word in paragraph J. means "afterthought"? _____

C. Return to Exercise A. Place two check marks (✔✔) in front of the word in COLUMN II that is the ANTONYM of the word in COLUMN I. Real aloud a complete sentence using this word.

D. Select one of the three (3) words (phrases) that best fulfills the MEANING of the sentence according to the narrative. Insert the words in the blank space. Read the completed sentence aloud.

1. Professor Stuart signed with the community college to_____.
   a. move   b. take a post   c. find a home

2. The Stuart family was happy because_____.
   a. of the new job   b. they moved   c. they got a home

3. The professor was glad when_____.
   a. he was with   b. he was at   c. he was offered
      the family   the college   a position

4. Knowing Lilian John's knowledge of Chinese _____.
   a. improved   b. prejudiced   c. excited

5. The Stuarts liked the neighborhood because_____.
   a. they liked   b. they bought   c. the Campbells
      the house   the house   were friends

6. The neighbors helped with the moving to_____.
   a. have great fun   b. detain the Stuarts   c. make moving easy

7. Mrs. Fox made the remark to show her _____ for foreigners.
   a. liking   b. dislike   c. love

8. The Campbells worried because the Stuarts were not _____
   to prejudice.
   a. neighbors   b. good   c. accustomed

9. An alien has to reside in the United States for five years to_____.
   a. become a citizen   b. buy a house   c. become prejudiced

10. Mrs. Campbell cried at the swearing-in ceremony because_____.
    a. she liked Lilian   b. she saw Mrs. Fox   c. she was unhappy

11. To celebrate Lilian's citizenship, the Stuarts planned_____.
    a. a big party   b. to go on a trip   c. to have a problem

12. Mrs. Fox was a problem because she_____.
    a. went on a trip.   b. was prejudiced   c. wouldn't come

13. Lilian planned the party during Mrs. Fox's absence to_____.
    a. have fun   b. celebrate with   c. give Mrs. Fox
                            other neighbors   a chance

14. Lilian was glad Mrs. Fox came to apologize because_____.
    a. the party was   b. she liked Mrs. Fox   c. she didn't
       a success   like parties

15. Mrs. Fox understood that to do a thing like this Lilian really_____.
    a. liked parties   b. liked people   c. didn't like people

16. To give someone a chance in this situation meant_____.
    a. to give a party   b. to like people   c. to save face

IX. Comprehension [Exercises)

A. Place a check mark (✔) in front of the correct response to each of the statements according to the narrative. Read the complete sentences aloud.

1. The Stuarts were happy because
   _____ a. the professor signed with the college.
   _____ b. they were moving.
   _____ c. they bought a house.

2. After John signed with the college
   _____ a. they gave a party.
   _____ b. they went to shop for a house.
   _____ c. they took a trip.

3. John met Lilian
   _____ a. when they were students at M.Y.U.
   _____ b. when he was in China.
   _____ c. when she visited in the United States.

4. The Stuarts went out to
   _____ a. move.
   _____ b. shop for a house.
   _____ c. plan a party.

5. They moved not far from
   _____ a. the Campbells.
   _____ b. the college.
   _____ c. the neighborhood.

6. The professor and Mr. Campbell studied
   _____ a. in China.
   _____ b. at M.Y.U.
   _____ c. law.

7. The neighbors helped the Stuarts
_____ a. at the college.
_____ b. with the party.
_____ c. with their moving.

8. Lilian planned a party to
_____ a. welcome Mrs. Fox.
_____ b. celebrate her citizenship.
_____ c. celebrate John's job.

9. The only problem was
_____ a. the neighbors.
_____ b. John's family.
_____ c. Mrs. Fox.

10. Lilian planned the party when
_____ a. the Foxes were away.
_____ b. the neighbors would come.
_____ c. the Campbells would come.

11. When the Foxes returned, Mrs. Fox
_____ a. came to talk with John.
_____ b. came to the party.
_____ c. came to apologize to Lilian.

12. Lilian wanted to give Mrs. Fox a chance to
_____ a. come to the party.
_____ b. save face.
_____ c. be present.

B. Below there are three (3) different thoughts in each of the exercises. Assign the proper sequence (order) of THOUGHT, according to the narrative, by numbering 1 to 3. Read aloud.

1. a. with the community college   _____
   b. when Professor Stuart   _____
   c. his family was happy   _____

2. a. had been looking   _____
    b. for a job since January   _____
    c. the professor   _____

3. a. while they were   _____
    b. John Stuart married Lilian _____
    c. students at M.Y.U.   _____

4. a. it was the second   _____
    b. for him   _____
    c. year of college   _____

5. a. as a minor subject   _____
    b. learning Chinese   _____
    c. John had been   _____

6. a. John's knowledge of   _____
    b. knowing Lilian improved   _____
    c. that difficult language   _____

7. a. he didn't speak   _____
    b. but John knew   _____
    c. as well as his wife   _____

8. a. to improve his knowledge   _____
    b. he was always trying hard _____
    c. of the language   _____

9. a. from the Campbells   _____
    b. a house was being sold   _____
    c. not far down the street   _____

10. a. than the   _____
    b. it was larger   _____
    c. Stuarts needed   _____

11. a. and more expensive than   _____
    b. they were able to afford   _____
    c. it was a big house   _____

12. a. meeting Mr. Campbell   _____
    b. besides, the professor had been   _____
    c. at social gatherings   _____

13. a. into their new home   _____
    b. the Stuarts moved   _____
    c. on a Sunday   _____

14. a. joined the Campbells in helping   _____
    b. the Stuarts with their moving   _____
    c. some of the neighbors   _____

15. a. stay out of   _____
    b. why don't these foreigners   _____
    c. our neighborhood   _____

16. a. the Campbells were worried   _____
    b. had been unaccustomed to prejudice _____
    c. about the Stuarts who   _____

17. a. her U.S. citizenship   _____
    b. Lilian received   _____
    c. on the twentieth of May   _____

18. a. a big neighborhood party   _____
    b. to celebrate Lilian's citizenship _____
    c. the Stuarts planned   _____

19. a. for a proper occasion   _____
    b. they had been waiting   _____
    c. to celebrate   _____

20. a. were going to be away   _____
    b. Lilian learned that the Foxes   _____
    c. on the twenty-seventh of May   _____

21. a. celebrating Lilian's new citizenship   _____
    b. the neighbors had been   _____
    c. throughout the night   _____

22. a. the new American   _____
    b. everyone was happy   _____
    c. to welcome   _____

23. a. on the following day   _____
    b. at the Stuarts' home   _____
    c. Mrs. Fox appeared   _____

24. a. you must really   _____
    b. to do a thing like this   _____
    c. care for people   _____

25. a. going to be   _____
    b. they were   _____
    c. friends now   _____

C. There are some statements listed below about the narrative. Write T for True in front of each statement that you think is true. Write F for False if the statement is not true. Read aloud.

_____ 1. Professor Stuart got a job, and his family was happy.
_____ 2. The professor had been looking for a job since February.
_____ 3. He was offered the position of a chairman.
_____ 4. The Stuarts had two sons.
_____ 5. Lilian was of Chinese descent.
_____ 6. They got married while they were students.
_____ 7. John learned Chinese as a major subject.
_____ 8. They bought a house not far from the Campbells.

_____ 9. The house was not very expensive.

_____ 10. The professor met Mr. Campbell at the University.

_____ 11. The Stuarts moved on Monday.

_____ 12. The neighbors helped them move.

_____ 13. Moving is easy.

_____ 14. The Campbells weren't worried about the Stuarts.

_____ 15. The Stuarts had been accustomed to prejudice.

_____ 16. Lilian received her citizenship in March.

_____ 17. Mr. Campbell sponsored Lilian.

_____ 18. The Stuarts planned a big party.

_____ 19. Mrs. Fox was no problem.

_____ 20. Lilian gave the party when the Foxes were home.

_____ 21. The party was a great success.

_____ 22. Everyone missed the Foxes.

_____ 23. Mrs. Fox came to apologize for missing the party.

_____ 24. Lilian was glad about Mrs. Fox's visit.

_____ 25. Mrs. Fox and Lilian were going to be friends.

_____ 26. Mrs. Fox embraced Lilian.

X. Composition and Discussion

A. In COLUMN I are the beginnings of sentences . In COLUMN II are the completions to sentences of COLUMN I . Select the completion best fitting each sentence in COLUMN I according to the narrative. Read the completed sentences orally. Compose new sentences orally and discuss the narrative.

COLUMN I	COLUMN II
1. The professor had been looking	a. for a proper occasion.
2. He was glad	b. about the Stuarts.
3. The Stuarts went out	c. while they were students.
4. John married Lilian	d. when he was offered a position.
5. Lilian was a student	e. for a job since January.
6. It was larger than	f. a great chore.
7. John and Lilian	g. you must really care for people.
8. Moving is always	h. what the Stuarts needed.

9.   Why don't these foreigners   i.   from China.
10. The Campbells were worried   j.   to welcome the new American.
11. Lilian received her citizenship   k.   a great success.
12. The Stuarts planned   l.   Mrs. Fox appeared at the Stuarts.
13. They had been waiting   m. to be friends now.
14. The party was   n.   to shop for a house.
15. Everyone was happy   o.   liked the neighborhood.
16. On the following day   p.   stay out of the neighborhood?
17. To do a thing like this   q.   on the twentieth of May.
18. They were going   r.   a big party to celebrate.

B. 1. Tell us about the neighborhood you live in.
   2. On what occasion would you celebrate?
   3. Do you like Lilian Stuart? Why?
   4. Do you like Mrs. Fox? Why?
   5. Describe the change in Mrs. Fox.
   6. Why was Lilian's plan to "save face" successful?

C. Read the poem aloud. Answer orally the questions listed following the poem.

Words

If I could express a thought the first time
I would refuse to repeat in vain
Were I able to cut down a tree at one stroke, [1]   [1] *blow of an ax*
I would stike but once.

But

When running the risk [2] *of being misunderstood,*   [2] *chance*
Or leaving things unaccomplished, [3]   [3] *not done*
I would spare [4] *neither words nor deeds.*   [4] *omit*

1. Why is the poem titled "Words"?

2. Read orally the lines containing "would." Explain their meaning.

3. Find *the + ordinal* and read orally the entire line.

4. How does line 3 of the first verse relate to line 3 of the second verse?

5. How does the first verse relate to the second verse? Discuss it in class.

6. Does the poem clearly convey the idea expressed in its title? Tell how it does, or how it doesn't.

D. Describe what you see in the picture below.

CHAPTER NINE

THE AMERICANS

IN THIS CHAPTER

Words to remember:

Relative Clauses— who, whom, which, whose, that, etc.

Relative Pronouns
as Subject—as Object
as Modifier of Noun

I. Narrative

A. Many people who wished to *seek* a new life sailed *across* the seven *seas* to the shores of the United States of America. More recently, the fastest jets *transport* the immigrants who come from almost every country of the earth to the United States. Though they are of *different nationalities, religions,* and *social classes,* they are *bound* by some *common goals.* Many come *in search* of *freedom* to worship, which they find here. Some look for food, others for fortune. For those who come, the United States of America is still the land of *opportunity.*

B. Some people look for the fertile land which they can settle on. Others seek a home in big and small cities of this *vast* country. They are

---

seek: look (for)
across: through
seas: ocean
transport: carry
different: diverse, not alike
nationalities: countries
religions: beliefs
social classes: ranks of people
bound: united
common: related
goals: intentions
in search: trying to find
freedom: liberty
opportunity: good chance
vast: great (size)
distances: land space
passports: document for travel
present: show
newcomers: recent arrivals
homeland: country of residence
altogether: completely
elements: principles

biased: prejudiced
opinions: views
tradition: heritage
ancient: very old
customs: habits
well-established: respected
similar: the same
background: environments
groups: communities
refused: declined
changes: differences
respect: regard with esteem
unlike: not the same as
own: themselves
birth: beginning
democracy: government by the people
suffer: endure, tolerate
used (to): accustomed (to)
leadership: guidance
tough: strong
toughness: strength
fellow man: people, persons

awed by the great *distances* that span the land. A person could travel three thousand miles across this country and no one asks questions. There are no borders to cross, no *passports* to *present*. The *newcomers* are happy with the people whom they meet in their new *homeland*. But this happiness is not *altogether* without some setbacks.

C. The same human *elements* which accompanied them to the New World became great obstacles. They brought with them *biased opinions*, old *traditions, ancient customs*, and quite a few *well-established* prejudices. People of *similar* national *backgrounds* settled close to each other. The German immigrants created their own neighborhoods, as did the Poles, the Italians, the Irish, and many other nationalities and ethnic *groups*. For the most part, they were tolerant of each other's religious beliefs. Though they met in their daily endeavors, most of them *refused* to allow their children to associate or intermarry.

D. But as the population increases, people come to live closer together. They learn to tolerate differences, and accept *changes*. They *respect* people whose backgrounds are *unlike* their *own*. They find it necessary to settle their differences peacefully, under the law of the land. Not everyone was born under equal circumstances. But every individual has the right to the "pursuit of his own happiness." This is an inalienable right to every American.

E. The Americans are proud people. They are proud of their heritage. They remember the Revolution and the *birth* of the Republic. They know that to live in a *democracy* means to *suffer* many sacrifices. The Americans are *used* to changes. They know how to make the best of a situation, and they adjust readily to changes.

F. Their president, whose authority they respect, will lead them. The Americans vote to elect their *leadership* in free elections. If their elected leaders prove untrustworthy, they will not stay in office. The people will not vote for them again.

G. The American people are hard-working and *tough*. But underneath that *toughness*, they are charitable. They are always ready to help their *fellow man.* This is the reason why so many come to the land called the United States of America. They, too, want to be called "Americans."

Idea Questions:

1. Why do many people come to the Untied States?

2. How do we feel freedom in the United States?

3. Why do people with similar backgrounds live close to each other?

4. How do people learn to accept changes?

5. How are people "equal" and how are they "not equal"?

6. Why are the Americans a proud people?

7. How did the Americans succeed?

8. How do the American people elect their leadership?

9. Why do we say "the Americans are tough"?

10. What is the MAIN IDEA of this narrative?

II. Words in Context [Pictographs]

Below are the words used in the narrative. Were possible, each word has a [synonym], or it is defined as used in the story. Where possible, an *(antonym)* is also given. Make up sentences about the pictographs choosing the words you need. Read aloud.

Example: [sail]= The immigrants traveled by boat.

A. and B.

Sail [**travel by boat**]; shore [**coastline**] *(ocean)*; recently [**lately**] *(long ago)*; immigrant [**settler**] *(emigrant)*; worship [**pray**] *(blaspheme)*; fortune [**wealth**] *(poverty)*; settle [**establish oneself**] *(move on)*; fertile [**fruitful**] *(arid)*; awe [**reverence**] *(irreverence)*; span [**extend**]; border [**boundary**] *(interior)*; setback [**obstacle**] *(advancement)*

Drawing of paragraphs A & B

C. and D.

Ethnic [**cultural**]; tolerant [**understanding**] *(intolerant)*; belief [**faith**] *(disbelief)*; endeavor [**work**] *(idleness)*; associate [**be friends**] *(disassociate)*; marry [**wed**] *(divorce)*; settle [**pacify**] *(unsettle)*; difference [**dissimilarity**] *(similarity)*; respect [**regard**] *(abuse)*; pursuit [**striving**] *(avoiding)*; inalienable [**indisputable**] *(disputable)*

E., F. and G.

proud [**self-satisfied**] *(ashamed)*; heritage [**tradition**]; sacrifice [**loss**] *(profit)*; [**adapt**] *(disturb)*; untrustworthy [**unreliable**] *(trustworthy)*; tough [**able to take adversity**] *(soft)*; underneath [**beneath**] *(above)*; charitable [**benevolent**] *(selfish)*

Drawing of paragraph C & D

III. Structures [Phrases]

Below are some PHRASES taken from the narrative. Make complete sentences and read them aloud.

1.	across	- come	- the		- seas
2.	from	- arrive	- every		- country
3.	in	- settle	- big		- cities
4.	across	- travel	- this		- country
5.	of	- people	- similar	- live	- background
6.	allow	- associate	- their		- children
7.	learn	- tolerate	- changes		- accept
8.	under	- born	- equal		- circumstances
9.	pursuit	- right	- of		- happiness
10.	tough	- Americans	- and	- be	- charitable

Drawing of paragraph E, F & G

IV. Sentences

A. Read the following sentences aloud. Repeat, substituting where possible, the synonym of the words in *italics*, or a phrase that explains the meaning. Make other necessary changes.

Example: *Recently*, they traveled by jet.
Lately, the settlers come by jet.

1. People wished to *seek* a new life.

2. They *sailed* across the seas.

3. The *immigrants* come from almost every country.

4. They are of different *nationalities*.

5. Many come in search of *freedom*.

6. Others look for *fortune*.

7. The United States is the land of *opportunity*.

8. Some settle on *fertile* land.

9. They are *awed* by the great distances.

10. There are no *borders* to cross.

11. The *newcomers* are happy.

12. But there are some *setbacks*.

13. They brought with them *ethnic* traditions.

14. They were *tolerant* of each other.

15. They had different *beliefs*.

16. People of different beliefs are *married* to each other.

17. They respect people of *different* backgrounds.

18. It is necessary to settle *differences*.

19. Not everyone was born under equal *circumstances*.

20. Everyone has the right to the *pursuit* of happiness.

21. The Americans are a *proud* people.

22. To live in a democracy means to suffer *sacrifices*.

23. People must *adjust* to a situation.

24. They are tough but *charitable*.

25. The *newcomers* want to be called "Americans."

B. Fill in the blanks with words from the narrative. Each space may be filled by a word or phrase. Do not refer back to the narrative. Where possible, use variations of the missing words. Read aloud.

Many people _____ wished to _____ a new life _____ across the seven _____. They sailed to the _____ of America. The _____ jets _____ the immigrants. They are _____ by some _____ goals. Many come in _____ of _____ to worship, _____ they find here. For those _____ come, the United States of America is _____ the land of _____.

Some people _____ on land _____ is fertile. They are _____ by the great _____ that span the land. A _____ could travel three thousand _____ across this _____ and no one _____ questions. There are no _____ to cross, no _____ to present.

The same human _____ which accompanied them to the _____ became great _____. People of _____ national _____ settled _____ to each. They were _____ of each other's _____ beliefs. But they refused to _____ their children to _____ or intermarry.

But as the _____ increases, people come to _____ closer _____. They _____ to _____ differences, and accept _____. They _____ people _____ backgrounds are _____ their own.

The Americans are a _____ people. They are proud of their _____. They remember the _____ and the _____ of the _____. They know _____ to live in a _____ means to _____ many _____. The Americans are _____ to _____ .

Their president _____ authority they _____ will _____ them. The Americans _____ to _____ their leadership in _____ elections. The Americans _____ are _____ working. But they are _____. They are always _____ to _____ their fellow _____. This is the _____ why so many come to this _____ called the _____ of _____.

V. Grammar (Points of Interest)

Relative Clauses Modifying Nouns. Two sentences may be combined when a noun in one sentence is identical with a noun in a second sentence. In such cases, a RELATIVE PRONOUN such as *who, whom, which, whose,* etc., will replace the noun in the second sentence when the two sentences are joined.

A. **Relative Pronoun** as **Subject**. In the following examples, the relative pronouns *who* (referring to persons), *which* (referring to things), or *that* (referring to persons or things) replace the noun (subject) in the second sentence.

1. Many people wished to seek a new life.
2. *People* sailed across the seven seas.

    (**who**)

3. Many people *who* wished to seek a new life sailed across the seven seas.

1. Jets transported the immigrants.
2. *The immigrants* came from almost every country.

    (**who**)

3. Jets transported the immigrants *who* came from almost every country.

1. Some people settle on land.
2. *The land* is very fertile.

    (**that**)

3. Some people settle on land *that* is very fertile.

B. **Relative Pronoun** as **Object**. In the following examples, the relative pronouns *whom*, *which*, or *that* replace the object of the second sentence.

1. The newcomers are happy with the people.
2. They meet *the people* in their new homeland.

    (**whom**)

3. The newcomers are happy with the people *whom* they meet in their new homeland.

1. Many come in search of freedom to worship.
2. They find *freedom to worship* here.
   (which)

3. Many come in search of freedom to worship *that* they find here.

1. Some people look for land to settle on.
2. They find *fertile land* to settle on.
   (that)

3. Some people look for fertile land *that* they can settle on.

Note: In conversation, the RELATIVE PRONOUN as OBJECT is often
       omitted. See third example below.

The people *whom* they met...   (formal)
The people *that* they met...   (informal)
The people they met...   (conversational)

C. **Relative Pronoun** as **Modifier of Noun.** In the following examples,
   the relative pronoun *whose* replaces the possessive form of a noun.

1. They respect people.
2. The *people's* background is unlike their own.
   (whose)

3. They respect people *whose* background is unlike their own.

1. The president will lead them.
2. They respect the *leader's* authority.
   (whose)

3. The president *whose* authority they respect will lead them.

VI. Word Recognition

A. Circle the word in Column II most *like* the word in Column I, and circle the word or phrase in Column II most *unlike* the word in Column I. This oral identification of words ought to be timed.

COLUMN I	COLUMN II	COLUMN III
1. **awe**	a. advice b. equality c. reverence	a. irreverence b. inequality c. deterrent
2. **charitable**	a. soft b. benevolent c. trustworthy	a. selfish b. tough c. able to take adversity
3. **endeavor**	a. dominate b. work c. advise	a. give up b. be idle c. conflict
4. **establish**	a. organize b. seek c. settle	a. move on b. find c. break up
5. **fertile**	a. complete b. private c. fruitful	a. arid b. careless c. public
6. **inalienable**	a. unreliable b. guilty c. indisputable	a. disputable b. innocent c. untrustworthy
7. **recently**	a. beyond b. lately c. farther	a. near b. long ago c. reasonable

8. **respect**
   a. regard
   b. divorce
   c. confuse

   a. dissimilarity
   b. difference
   c. abuse

9. **setback**
   a. obstacle
   b. border
   c. belief

   a. interior
   b. advancement
   c. disbelief

10. **shore**
    a. sail
    b. travel
    c. coastline

    a. ocean
    b. space
    c. span

B. In the space on the left write the word(s) that best fit the expression in **bold print**. Make other necessary changes. Read aloud.

_____ 1. People **travel by boat.**

_____ 2. **Lately**, they come by jet.

_____ 3. They seek freedom to **pray.**

_____ 4. Some **establish themselves** on land.

_____ 5. The land is **fruitful.**

_____ 6. There are no **boundaries.**

_____ 7. There were some **obstacles.**

_____ 8. People remember their **cultural** background.

_____ 9. Many don't **fraternize** with one another.

_____ 10. They make the best of the **situation.**

_____ 11. The Americans are **self-satisfied.**

_____ 12. They remember their **tradition.**

_____ 13. Much is **surrendered** in democracy.

_____ 14. The Americans **adapt** well.

_____ 15. The Americans are **firm.**

_____ 16. But they are **benevolent.**

VII. Concept Recognition

Fill in the word (phrase) most fitting to express the CONCEPT of the sentence according to the narrative. Read the completed sentence aloud.

A. People sailed to the United States of America to seek _____.
    1. counsel
    2. a new life
    3. their relatives
    4. the seven seas

B. They were bound by _____.
    1. some common goals
    2. the fastest jets
    3. every country
    4. different nationalities

C. They were awed by _____.
    1. the land
    2. the small cities
    3. the great distances
    4. the fertile land

D. A person could travel across the three thousand miles, and there were _____.
    1. no boundaries
    2. passports to cross
    3. happy people
    4. unhappy people

E. Even though the people were happy, there were _____.
    1. questions
    2. some setbacks
    3. answers
    4. similar backgrounds

F. People of similar national backgrounds settled _____.
    1. on land
    2. in the cities
    3. close to each other
    4. far from each other

G. Some people settled close to each other because they were of _____ national backgrounds.
    1. similar
    2. different
    3. profound
    4. least

H. They refused to allow their children to associate because they

_____.

1. were Americans
3. were immigrants
2. had different beliefs
4. were tolerant

I. People live closer together when _____.
1. the population increases
3. their differences are greater
2. their backgrounds are different
4. they like their neighbors

J. Everyone has the right to _____.
1. live in the United States
3. live in the city
2. live on land
4. the pursuit of happiness

K. In a democracy much is _____.
1. done
3. forgotten
2. needed
4. sacrificed

L. The Americans are proud, but they are also _____.
1. leaders
3. elected
2. charitable
4. ready

M. Because they are used to changes, the Americans know how to

_____.

1. be kind
3. elect their president
2. make the best of a situation
4. work hard

VIII. *Telling the Meaning*

A. Place a check mark (✔) in front of the word in COLUMN II that best fits the MEANING of the word in COLUMN I. Read aloud a complete sentence using this word.

COLUMN I   COLUMN II

1. **adjust**
   _____ a. surrender
   _____ b. sacrifice
   _____ c. adapt

2. **belief**
   _____ a. faith
   _____ b. fortune
   _____ c. disbelief

3. **border**
   _____ a. interior
   _____ b. boundary
   _____ c. land

4. **ethnic**
   _____ a. biased
   _____ b. national
   _____ c. cultural

5. **fortune**
   _____ a. poverty
   _____ b. income
   _____ c. wealth

6. **fruitful**
   _____ a. orderly
   _____ b. fertile
   _____ c. arid

7. **immigrant**
   _____ a. settler
   _____ b. emigrant
   _____ c. traveler

8. **obstacle**
   - _____ a. span
   - _____ b. setback
   - _____ c. advancement

9. **ocean**
   - _____ a. shore
   - _____ b. coastline
   - _____ c. ground

10. **proud**
    - _____ a. tough
    - _____ b. ashamed
    - _____ c. charitable

B. Pick the right expression. Complete the following sentences with the word that best fits the situation. Read aloud.

recently	tolerant	endeavor
sail	worship	settle
pursuit	proud	heritage
in search	altogether	elements

1. When you talk about human principles, you're talking about human
   _____ .
2. If you're trying to find a place to live, you're going _____ of a place.
3. Freedom to pray means freedom to _____.
4. When a person is understanding, he is a _____ person.
5. Those people who arrived here lately came _____.

C. Select one of the three (3) words (phrases) that best fulfills the MEANING of the sentence according to the narrative. Insert the word in the blank space. Read the completed sentences aloud.

1. The immigrants came to the United States to seek _____.
   a. a new life   b. poverty   c. obstacles

2. The immigrants fly on jets to arrive _____.
   a. faster   b. in the city   c. on land

3. There are many different nationalities, but there are some _____.
   a. good people   b. poor immigrants   c. common goals

4. The immigrants settle on land because they know it is _____.
   a. arid   b. fertile   c. vast

5. The people are awed by the great _____ that _____ the land.
   a. distances, span   b. homes, grow   c. opportunity, travels

6. The people can travel far because there are no _____ to cross.
   a. borders   b. questions   c. passports

7. There were some _____ in the New World.
   a. newcomers   b. obstacles   c. elements

8. The immigrants settled close to each other because of _____ national backgrounds.
   a. different   b. similar   c. prejudiced

9. The newcomers believed that their children should stay in their own _____ group.
   a. age   b. ethnic   c. intelligence

10. They would not allow their children to _____ outside their group, or to _____.
    a. play, study   b. associate,   c. settle, travel
                        intermarry

11. People come to live closer together because _____.
    a. they like each other   b. they like to travel   c. population increases

12. Because people live closer together, they learn to _____.
    a. worship together   b. play together   c. tolerate differences

13. They find it necessary to _____ their _____ peacefully.
    a. settle, differences   b. play, games   c. plan, vacations

14. People respect each other because everyone has the right to the
    _____.
    a. equal circumstances b. pursuit of   c. same fortune
                               happiness

15. Even though this is a democracy, there are many _____ to be made.
    a. sacrifices   b. fortunes   c. situations

16. In changing situations, people must get used to _____.
    a. fortunes   b. adjustments   c. bad leadership

17. When a leader proves untrustworthy, the Americans _____.
    a. will not keep him   b. will vote for him   c. will elect him

18. The Americans are tough and hard-working, but they don't forget
    to _____.
    a. play   b. help their   c. make a fortune
                               fellowman

IX. Comprehension (Exercises)

A. Place a check mark (✔) in front of the correct statements according
   to the narrative. Read the completed sentences aloud.

1. Many people sailed across the seas
   _____ a. for no reason at all.
   _____ b. to seek a new life.
   _____ c. to seek common friends.

2. The immigrants are bound by
   _____ a. common religion.
   _____ b. common social classes.
   _____ c. common goals.

3. For most newcomers, America is
_____ a. the land of opportunity.
_____ b. the land to worship.
_____ c. the land of common goals.

4. Some people settle on land because it is
_____ a. very fertile.
_____ b. very vast.
_____ c. very arid.

5. The newcomers are awed by the
_____ a. many cities.
_____ b. many people.
_____ c. great distances.

6. One could travel three thousand miles across this country and
_____ a. there are no borders.
_____ b. there are no people.
_____ c. there are no fortunes.

7. Though the people are happy, there are
_____ a. many children.
_____ b. many cities.
_____ c. some setbacks.

8. People of similar national backgrounds settled
_____ a. with the other groups.
_____ b. on land.
_____ c. close to each other.

9. Though they were different, they
_____ a. learned to tolerate each other.
_____ b. learned to play with each other.
_____ c. refused to talk to each other.

10. Because of ethnic differences they refused to

    _____ a. settle on land.

    _____ b. play games.

    _____ c. allow their children to intermarry.

11. People came to live closer together because

    _____ a. population increased.

    _____ b. they liked each other.

    _____ c. they liked their children.

12. People are not born under equal circumstances, but

    _____ a. they have equal rights.

    _____ b. they can emigrate.

    _____ c. they can live on land.

13. To live in a democracy means to

    _____ a. live free and easy.

    _____ b. suffer many sacrifices.

    _____ c. change.

14. People make the best of a situation when

    _____ a. they are equal.

    _____ b. they live together.

    _____ c. they adjust to changes.

15. Though the Americans are tough, they

    _____ a. help others.

    _____ b. don't like the immigrants.

    _____ c. don't help others.

B. Below there are three (3) different thoughts expressed in each of the exercises. Assign the proper sequence (order) of THOUGHT, according to the narrative, by numbering 1 to 3. Read aloud.

1. a. who wished to seek a new life   _____

    b. many people   _____

    c. sailed across the seven seas   _____

2. a. transport the immigrants   _____
    b. to the United States   _____
    c. the fastest jets   _____

3. a. of freedom to worship   _____
    b. many come in search   _____
    c. that they find here   _____

4. a. the United States of America is   _____
    b. for those who come   _____
    c. still the land of opportunity   _____

5. a. in big and small cities   _____
    b. of this vast land   _____
    c. some people seek a home   _____

6. a. that span the land   _____
    b. they are awed   _____
    c. by the great distances   _____

7. a. with the people whom   _____
    b. they met in their new homeland   _____
    c. the newcomers were happy   _____

8. a. without some setbacks   _____
    b. was not altogether   _____
    c. but this happiness   _____

9. a. national backgrounds   _____
    b. people of similar   _____
    c. settled close to each other   _____

10. a. each other's religious beliefs   _____
    b. for the most part,   _____
    c. they were tolerant of   _____

11. a. increases, people come   _____
    b. to live closer together   _____
    c. but as the population   _____

12. a. differences, and   _____
    b. they learn to tolerate   _____
    c. accept changes   _____

13. a. not everyone   _____
    b. under equal circumstances   _____
    c. was born   _____

14. a. but every individual   _____
    b. pursuit of his own happiness   _____
    c. has the right to the   _____

15. a. live in a democracy means   _____
    b. they know that to   _____
    c. to suffer many sacrifices   _____

16. a. the best of a situation, and   _____
    b. they know how to make   _____
    c. they adjust easily to changes   _____

17. a. will lead them   _____
    b. their president whose   _____
    c. authority they respect   _____

18. a. in free elections   _____
    b. to elect their leadership   _____
    c. the Americans vote   _____

19. a. they are   _____
    b. underneath that toughness   _____
    c. charitable   _____

20. a. ready to help   _____
    b. they are always   _____
    c. their fellow man   _____

21. a. so many come to this land   _____
    b. this is the reason why   _____
    c. called the United States of America   _____

22. a. to be called   _____
    b. they, too, want   _____
    c. Americans   _____

C. There are some statements listed below about the narrative. Write **T** for **True** in front of each statement that you think is true. Write **F** for **False** in front of each statement that you think is not true. Read aloud.

_____ 1. All people come to the United States to make a fortune.
_____ 2. They come from almost every country.
_____ 3. People of different nationalities come to the United States.
_____ 4. The immigrants have one common goal.
_____ 5. America is the land of opportunity for many.
_____ 6. The land in the United States is very fertile.
_____ 7. The people are awed by the great fortune.
_____ 8. They cannot travel far because of borders.
_____ 9. The immigrants must carry passports to travel in the United States.
_____ 10. The newcomers are happy with the people they meet.
_____ 11. Their happiness has some setbacks.
_____ 12. The immigrants brought with them some prejudices.
_____ 13. People of different national backgrounds settle close to each other.
_____ 14. For the most part, they are tolerant of each other.
_____ 15. But the immigrants refuse to allow their children to intermarry.
_____ 16. People come to live closer together when population increases.

_____ 17. They do not respect people who are unlike their own.

_____ 18. They settle their differences peacefully.

_____ 19. Everyone was born under equal circumstances.

_____ 20. Everyone has the right to the pursuit of his happiness.

_____ 21. The Americans are proud people.

_____ 22. To live in a democracy means to suffer sacrifices.

_____ 23. The Americans are not used to changes.

_____ 24. They make the best of a situation.

_____ 25. A respected leader will lead them.

_____ 26. There are free elections.

_____ 27. People will not vote for an untrustworthy leader.

_____ 28. The Americans are hard working.

_____ 29. They are tough, but charitable.

_____ 30. The Americans help their fellow man.

X. Composition and Discussion

A. In COLUMN I are the beginnings of sentences. In COLUMN II are the completions to sentences of COLUMN I. Select the completion in COLUMN II best fitting each sentence in COLUMN I according to the narrative. Read the completed sentences orally. Compose new sentences orally and discuss the narrative.

COLUMN I	COLUMN II
1. Many people sailed	a. under equal circumstances.
2. The fastest jets	b. used to changes.
3. Some look for food	c. hard-working and tough.
4. Some people settle on land	d. to help their fellow man.
5. They are awed by the	e. others for fortune.
6. There are no borders to cross	f. and accept changes.
7. This happiness was not altogether	g. of each other's beliefs.
8. They brought with them	h. no passports to present.
9. People of similar backgrounds	i. across the seven seas.
10. They were tolerant	j. that is very fertile.
11. As the population increases	k. great distances that span the land.

12. They learn to tolerate differences   l. people come to live closer together.

13. Not everyone was born   m. settled close to each other.

14. The Americans are   n. well-established prejudices.

15. The American people are   o. without some setbacks.

16. They are always ready   p. transport the immigrants.

B. 1. Tell us about your most memorable trip.
2. Why did you travel?
3. Describe the circumstances in your country.
4. Tell us what you think about the people you met.
5. Tell us how you adjusted to the changes.
6. Tell us what you think about helping others.

C. Tell us what you think when I say :

immigrant - the United States of America - prejudice - land of opportunity - tradition - nationality - work - tough - kind - equal rights - revolution - elections

D. Read the poem aloud. Answer orally the questions listed following the poem.

Poverty [1]   [1]being poor
How poor, indeed [2]*, is he who*   [2]truly
has the means [3] *to make*   [3]way
his dreams come true
in time to hear a wish [4]*!*   [4]desire
Can you compare the riches [5]   [5]wealth
of forgotten fable-lands
to dreams that slowly
become reality?
How poor, indeed, is he who
knows no peace of spirit [6]*, nor*   [6]mind
the blessing [7] *of a wish that he*   [7]benediction
can shout [8] *at time and space...*   [8]yell

*Can he compare the
riches of his wasted⁹ days
to dreams that slowly
come to be?*

⁹spent in vain

1. Read orally the verses where you find related words to the title of the poem.
2. Read orally the verses where you find antonyms of the title.
3. Explain the meaning of the first verse. Discuss it in class.
4. What is the meaning of the first two lines of the third verse? Discuss it in class.
5. Does the poem express poverty or wealth, or both? Discuss it in class.

E. Describe what you see in the picture below.

CHAPTER TEN

NEWS GAZETTE

IN THIS CHAPTER

Office collects lost articles
of careless college students

Words to remember:
this, that, these, those

RELATIVE PRONOUN
whom, which, that

ADVERB-ADVERBIAL PHRASE
where - when

I. Narrative

A. The person to whom he was speaking was a young college *freshman.* Mr. Ungerer, the director of student *activities,* was serious. "I can't understand why most of the students leave things lying around." He *pointed* in the *direction* of a large *box.* "Do you see that box? It's full of *lost* and *found* articles." The lost and found office on the first floor of the Administration Building has *collected* many lost *items.* This is the place where they are *kept.*

B. Mr. Ungerer said students are *advised* to put *identifying* marks on their books. "They ought to put the marks where you can see them. This way items would be returned to the owner quickly."

C. "Some students say that if they put their names on their books it will *lower* the *resale* value of their books," he added. "But that's ridiculous!"

D. Another factor leading to lost items is that students *trust* everyone. "Talk does little to *warn* the students," Ungerer continued. "We carry

---

freshman: beginning student
activities: functions, pursuits
pointed: singled out, showed
direction: toward
box: container, carton
lost: left behind
found: recovered
collected: gather
items: articles
kept: held
advised: counseled
identifying: recognition
lower: reduce
resale: sell back
trust: believe
warn: caution
discussions: talks
check: examine

gone: lost
offered: gave
pass it on: tell it
worth: valued
advantage: make the best (of it)
anticipate: expect
delay: postpone
toward: to (in time)
aim: try
enjoy: get pleasure (from)
equally: the same way
suggestions: ideas, hints
concerning: in regard (to)
feel free: don't hesitate
capacity: the maximum
recently: not long ago
crowds: numbers of people
in touch: close

our *discussions* to a point where a decision must be made. The students must make this decision. They must care for their possessions." Mr. Ungerer gave some further advice. If a student loses an item, the student should *check* the area where the item was lost. If the item is *gone*, check with the lost and found office. Keep checking with the lost and found office. Ungerer said he has hundreds of dollars worth of books and clothing that have never been claimed.

E. This reporter is glad she was there at the time Ungerer *offered* his advice. Now we *pass it on* to you, the student, for what it may be *worth*. Take *advantage* of it!

The Letter

September 21, 2011

Dear David:

F. *Because of some urgent work that I did not* anticipate, *I had to* delay *this letter. I know you've been waiting impatiently for the manuscript which I promised to send. It is almost finished now. The person to whom I'll send it is Bruce. You've instructed me to forward it to him. I understand the publication date* toward *which we* aim *is the fifteenth of January.*

G. *I want you to know that it was great fun to write this book. I can only hope that the students will* enjoy *it* equally. *If you have any* suggestions *to* make *concerning* the manuscript, *please* feel free to do so.

H. *The other night we went to the restaurant where we ate with you. Do you remember the place? "Alonso's." Of course, our conversation was about how much you've enjoyed eating there. The restaurant was* filled *to* capacity. *You were there with us at the time when the place had only* recently *opened. The* crowds *were smaller then. It's nothing important. I only wanted you to know that we always remember you.*

I. *Take good care. Give my regards to Weldon, Bruce, and all our friends. The very best to you from the family. Keep in touch.*

J. *With kindest regards.*

Cordially,
Bill

Idea Questions:

Lost and Found

1. Why was Mr. Ungerer serious?
2. Do the students always follow the advice of the director?
3. Why is it necessary to put identifying marks on books?
4. Why don't the students like marking their books?
5. Why isn't it a good idea to trust everyone?
6. What is the MAIN IDEA of this story?

The Letter

1. Why is Bill writing the letter to David?
2. Why is the letter written so late?
3. What is Bill remembering?
4. What is the MAIN IDEA in writing a letter to a friend?

II. Words in Context *[Pictographs]*

Below are some of the words used in the news article and the letter. Where possible, each word has a [**synonym**], or it is defined as used in the story. Where possible, an *(antonym)* is also given. Make up sentences about the pictographs choosing the words you need. Read aloud.

Example : [**serious**] = They spoke in earnest.

A. serious [**earnest**] *(funny)*; around [**about**]; full [**filled**] *(empty)*; article [**thing**]; collect [**gather**] *(distribute)*; mark [**sign**]; value [**worth**] *(uselessness)*; ridiculous [**not sensible**] *(serious)*; factor [**element**]; decision [**determination**] *(indecision)*; possession [**belonging**]; claim [**identify as one's own**] *(disclaim)*

B. urgent [**important**] *(unimportant)*; impatient [**restless**] *(patient)*; manuscript [**book**]; promise [**pledge**]; forward [**send**] *(keep)*; publication date [**date the finished book is offered to the public**]

Drawing of Lost and Found

III. Structures [Phrases]

Below are some PHRASES taken from the news article and the letter. Make complete sentences and read them aloud.

OFFICE COLLECTS LOST ARTICLES

1.	of	- lost	- careless	- found	- students
2.	person		- to	- speak	- whom
3.	of	- director	- student		- activities
4.	things		- lying	- leave	- around
5.	identifying		- marks		- put
6.	to	- return	- the		- owner
7.	the	- lower	- resale		- value
8.	to		- lost		- items

Drawing of the Letter

9. a   - decision   - point   - make   - where
10. the   - lost   - area   - check   - where

THE LETTER

1. because   - urgent   - of   - some   - work
2. delay   - I   - this   - had   - letter
3. the   - aim   - publication - toward   - date
4. the   - go   - other   - restaurant - night   - where
5. the   - be   -best   - our   - to you
6. very   - family

IV. Sentences

A. Read the following sentences aloud. Repeat, substituting where possible, the synonym of the word in italics.

Example : There were items lying *around.*
There were items lying *about.*

1. The director was *serious.*
2. He *pointed* to a large box.
3. The *box* was full of lost and found articles.
4. The office has *collected* many items.
5. Put your *marks* where you can see them.
6. It will *lower* the resale value.
7. Talk does little to *warn* students.
8. A *decision* must be made.
9. They must care for their *possessions.*
10. Mr. Ungerer *gave* us some advice.
11. The student should *check* the area.
12. We *pass it on* to you.
13. 1 did not *anticipate* urgent work.
14. You've been waiting *impatiently.*
15. The person to whom I'll send the *manuscript* is Bruce.
16. You've instructed me to *forward* it to him.
17. The students will enjoy it *equally.*
18. *Feel free* to make suggestions.
19. We *conversed* about you.
20. The restaurant was filled to *capacity.*
21. The place was only *recently* opened.

B. Fill in the blanks with words from the readings. Each space may be filled by a word or phrase. Do not refer back to the narrative. Where possible, use variations of the missing words. Read aloud.

The person to _____ he was speaking was a _____ college freshman. The _____ of _____ activities was _____. He pointed in the direction of a large_____. This is the place_____ they are_____.

Mr. Ungerer, director of student_____, said students are _____ to put _____ marks on their _____. "They ought to _____ the marks _____ you can _____ them."

Students _____ everyone. "We carry our _____ to a point _____a decision must be _____. The students must _____ this. They must _____ for their _____."

The students should _____ the area the item was _____. Keep _____ with the _____and _____ office.

This reporter is _____she was _____at the _____ Ungerer _____ his_____. Now we _____ it on to _____. Take _____!

_____David:

Because of _____ urgent work _____ I did not_____, I had to this. I know you've been _____ impatiently for the _____ which I promised to _____. It is _____ finished now. The person to _____I'll send it is Bruce. I understand the publication _____ toward _____ we aim is the fifteenth of _____.

    It was great _____ to write this. I can only _____that the _____ will _____ it.

    The other _____ we went to the restaurant _____ we ate with you. Do you _____ the place? I know, you've _____ eating there. The restaurant was _____ to _____. I only wanted you to _____ that we always _____ you.

    Take care. Give my _____ to Weldon, Bruce, and all our _____. The very _____ to you from the _____. Keep in _____.

With _____ regards,

V. Grammar (Points of Interest)

A. The **Relative Pronouns** *whom, which,* or *that* may replace the object of the preposition.

1. The *person* is a young college freshman.
2. He was speaking to *this person*.
      (whom)

3. The person/to *whom* he was speaking/was a young college freshman.

1. There was a *large box*.
2. He pointed in *the direction* of a large box.
      (which)

3. The direction/in *which* he pointed/was a large box.

NOTE : In informal speech that is often substituted for which. The preposition stands after the verb or object. The **relative pronoun** is often omitted in conversation.

The person *(that)* he was talking to was a young college freshman.

In the direction *(that)* he pointed was a large box.

B. The **Relative Pronoun** *where* often replace an **adverb** or **adverbial phrase** indicating location.

1. This is the *place*.
2. They are kept in *this place*.
      (where)

3. This is the place *where* they are kept.

1. We carry our discussions to a point.
2. *At this point* a decision must be made.

        (where)

3. We carry our discussions to a point *where* a decision must be made.

1. The student should check the area.
2. The item was lost in *this area.*

        (where)

3. The student should check the area *where* the item was lost.

Note : An **adverb** or **adverbial phrase** may be replaced by the **relative pronoun** *when.*

1. You were there with us at the time.
2. The place was opened *at that time.*

        (when)

3. You were there with us at the time *when* the place was opened.

VI. Word Recognition

A. Circle the word(s) in Column II most *like* that in Column I, and circle the word(s) in Column III most *unlike* the word in Column I. This oral identification of words ought to be timed.

COLUMN I	COLUMN II	COLUMN III
1. **claim**	a. notice b. identify as one's own c. move	a. disclaim b. neglect c. rest

2. **collect**
   - a. accept
   - b. gather
   - c. attend

   - a. carry
   - b. sell
   - c. distribute

3. **full**
   - a. filled
   - b. easy
   - c. wary

   - a. idle
   - b. late
   - c. empty

4. **impatient**
   - a. perfect
   - b. restless
   - c. private

   - a. patient
   - b. spacious
   - c. public

5. **ridiculous**
   - a. insignificant
   - b. not sensible
   - c. easy-going

   - a. innocent
   - b. funny
   - c. serious

6. **serious**
   - a. good
   - b. earnest
   - c. eager

   - a. lazy
   - b. unable
   - c. funny

7. **urgent**
   - a. important
   - b. clamorous
   - c. public

   - a. devious
   - b. simple
   - c. unimportant

8. **value**
   - a. worth
   - b. endeavor
   - c. factor

   - a. habit
   - b. idleness
   - c. uselessness

B. In the space on the left write the word(s) that would best fit the expression in bold print. Make other necessary changes. Read aloud.

_____ 1. The director was **earnest**.
_____ 2. The students leave things lying **about**.
_____ 3. There are many lost **items**.
_____ 4. We **gather** the items here.
_____ 5. The students must **sign** their books.

_____ 6. One must value one's **possessions**.

_____ 7. You should **claim** the articles.

_____ 8. The matter is **pressing**.

_____ 9. 1 know you are **impatient**.

_____ 10. I'll **send** it, as I promised.

VII. Concept Recognition

Fill in the most appropriate word (phrase) to express the CONCEPT of the sentence according to the readings. Read the completed sentence aloud.

A. The director was speaking to a student about _____.
1. lost items
2. activities
3. lying around
4. a large box

B. The director pointed to a box which was full of _____.
1. student activities
2. lost and found items
3. college freshmen
4. persons

C. He advised students to mark their books so that they would be _____ to the owner quickly.
1. put
2. kept
3. returned
4. valued

D. Students don't put marks in their books because this would _____.
1. be returned
2. be kept
3. mark the book
4. lower the resale value

E. Talk does little to warn students because they _____.
1. trust everybody
2. have many books
3. don't care
4. are the owners

F. The director can give advice, but the students must make the _____.
1. possession
2. decision
3. loss
4. warning

G. Students don't care for their lost items enough to _____ with the office.
  1. decide
  2. trust
  3. check
  4. advise

H. Many items remain in the lost and found office _____.
  1. claimed
  2. unclaimed
  3. checked
  4. dated

I. The reporter was glad to talk to the director because she could _____ the other students about it.
  1. tell
  2. claim
  3. take advantage
  4. point

VIII. Telling the Meaning

A. Place a check mark (✔) in front of the word in Column II that best fits the MEANING of the word in Column I. Read aloud a complete sentence using this word.

COLUMN I   COLUMN II

1. **about**
  _____ a. empty
  _____ b. around
  _____ c. earnest

2. **claim**
  _____ a. disclaim
  _____ b. possess
  _____ c. identify as one's own

3. **comic**
  _____ a. incriminating
  _____ b. serious
  _____ c. ridiculous

4. **decision**
   _____ a. determination
   _____ b. indecision
   _____ c. celebration

5. **declaration**
   _____ a. trust
   _____ b. publication
   _____ c. secrecy

6. **demand**
   _____ a. disclaim
   _____ b. claim
   _____ c. detain

7. **determination**
   _____ a. indecision
   _____ b. decision
   _____ c. distrust

8. **earnest**
   _____ a. serious
   _____ b. funny
   _____ c. responsible

9. **gather**
   _____ a. collect
   _____ b. gain
   _____ c. distribute

B. Recognize words in the Narrative.

1. Which word in paragraph A. means "beginning student"? _____
2. Which word in paragraph A. means "singled out"? _____
3. Which word in paragraph A. means "recovered"? _____
4. Which word in paragraph A. means "left behind"? _____
5. Which word in paragraph E. means "make the best of it"? _____

C. Select one of the three (3) words (phrases) that best fulfills the MEANING of the sentence according to the readings. Insert the word in the blank space. Read the completed sentence aloud.

1. The director spoke to a _____college freshman.
   a. young   b. person   c. friendly

2. The director was _____ when he spoke.
   a. happy   b. amicable   c. serious

3. He pointed to a box full of _____.
   a. books   b. lost and found articles   c. marks

4. The lost and found office _____ items.
   a. collects   b. loses   c. sends

5. Students lose articles because they don't put _____ in them.
   a. money   b. marks   c. books

6. They ought to put the marks where you could _____ them.
   a. keep   b. lower   c. see

7. It lowers the resale value of books when students write their _____ on them.
   a. story   b. marks   c. names

8. Many items are lost because the students _____ everybody.
   a. see   b. like   c. trust

9. Only the students can make a _____ to _____ for their possessions.
   a. decision, care   b. discussion, talk   c. point, carry

10. There are always many items in the office which the students don't _____.
    a. claim   b. see   c. lose

IX. Comprehension [Exercises]

A. Place a check mark (✔) in front of the correct answer to each of the questions according to the readings. Read the complete reply aloud.

1. To whom was the director speaking?
   _____ a. to a young college freshman
   _____ b. to a professor
   _____ c. to a lady

2. Why was the director serious?
   _____ a. because he was talking
   _____ b. because the student listened
   _____ c. because students leave things lying around

3. What was in the box?
   _____ a. it was full of lost and found articles
   _____ b. it was full of books
   _____ c. it was full of students

4. Where was the lost and found office?
   _____ a. in the Administration Building
   _____ b. at the house
   _____ c. at the activities

5. Why should students put identifying marks on their books?
   _____ a. to lower the resale value
   _____ b. to have them returned quickly
   _____ c. to trust everyone

6. Is it useful to warn students?
   _____ a. yes, it is
   _____ b. no, it's useless
   _____ c. yes, it's useless

7. Who must make the decision?
   _____ a.   the director
   _____ b.   the college
   _____ c.   the student

8. Why are there so many items in the lost and found?
   _____ a.   because they keep everything there
   _____ b.   because students don't claim their possessions
   _____ c.   because students are glad

9. Why was Bill late in writing the letter to David?
   _____ a.   because of some urgent work
   _____ b.   because he forgot
   _____ c.   because he wrote to Bruce

10. What did Bill promise to do for David?
   _____ a.   he promised to write a letter
   _____ b.   he promised to send the manuscript
   _____ c.   he promised to call him

11. What is Bill asking for?
   _____ a.   he asks for the book
   _____ b.   he asks for suggestions
   _____ c.   he asks for more time

12. What can David expect soon?
   _____ a.   the restaurant
   _____ b.   the manuscript
   _____ c.   the call

13. In what way did Bill remember David?
   _____ a.   because Bill ate at the restaurant
   _____ b.   because Bill thought about David
   _____ c.   because Bill talked about David

14. What was it that Bill wanted David to know?

_____ a. that they ate at the restaurant

_____ b. that they thought about him

_____ c. that he would call David

B. Below there are three (3) different thoughts expressed in each of the exercises. Assign the proper sequence (order) of THOUGHT, according to the readings, by numbering 1 to 3. Read aloud.

1. a. the person to whom   _____
   b. a young college freshman _____
   c. he was speaking was   _____

2. a. of student activities   _____
   b. the director   _____
   c. was serious   _____

3. a. the direction of   _____
   b. a large box   _____
   c. he pointed in   _____

4. a. place where the articles _____
   b. this is the   _____
   c. are kept   _____

5. a. they ought to put   _____
   b. you could see them   _____
   c. the marks where   _____

6. a. be returned to   _____
   b. this way items would   _____
   c. the owner quickly   _____

7. a. lost items is that   _____
   b. another factor leading to _____
   c. students trust everyone   _____

8. a. to a point where   _____
   b. a decision must be made   _____
   c. we carry our discussions   _____

9. a. check the area where   _____
   b. the student should   _____
   c. the item was lost   _____

10. a. check with the   _____
   b. lost and found office   _____
   c. if the item is gone,   _____

11. a. of dollars worth of books   _____
   b. Ungerer said he has hundreds   _____
   c. and clothing that have never been claimed   _____

12. a. this reporter is glad   _____
   b. Ungerer offered his advice   _____
   c. she was there at the time   _____

13. a. that I did not anticipate   _____
   b. because of some urgent work   _____
   c. I had to delay this letter   _____

14. a. I'll send it   _____
   b. the person to whom   _____
   c. is Bruce   _____

15. a. toward which we aim   _____
   b. the publication date   _____
   c. is the fifteenth of January   _____

16. a. it was great fun   _____
   b. I want you to know that   _____
   c. to write this book   _____

284 • LET'S READ

17. a. that the students   _____
    b. will enjoy it equally   _____
    c. I can only hope   _____

18. a. to make concerning the manuscript,   _____
    b. if you have any suggestions   _____
    c. please feel free to do so   _____

19. a. to the restaurant   _____
    b. the other night we went   _____
    c. where we ate with you   _____

20. a. at the time when   _____
    b. you were with us   _____
    c. the place was only recently opened _____

C. There are some statements listed below about the readings. Write **T** for **True** in front of each statement that you think is true. Write **F** for **False** if the statement is not true.

Read aloud.

_____ 1. The director was speaking to his friend.

_____ 2. The director was serious.

_____ 3. Students leave things lying about.

_____ 4. There were many items in the box.

_____ 5. The lost and found office is at home.

_____ 6. Students put identifying marks on books.

_____ 7. Students trust nobody.

_____ 8. The decision must be made by the director.

_____ 9. Students should check with the lost and found.

_____ 10. Students come to claim their possessions.

_____ 11. The reporter is glad to listen to Ungerer.

_____ 12. Bill forgot to write to David.

_____ 13. David was waiting for the manuscript.

_____ 14. The manuscript is almost finished.

_____ 15. It was fun to write this book.

_____ 16. When Bill went to the restaurant, it was filled to capacity.

_____ 17. He talked about Dave.

X. Composition and Discussion

A. In Column I are the beginnings of sentences. In Column II are the completions to the sentences of Column I. Select the completion best fitting each sentence in Column I according to the readings. Read the completed sentences orally. Compose new sentences orally and discuss.

COLUMN I

1. He was speaking
2. The director
3. He pointed in the direction
4. This is the place
5. Talk does little
6. The student must
7. The student should check
8. I had to delay
9. It was great fun
10. I only wanted you to know

COLUMN II

a. where the articles are kept.
b. of a large box.
c. to write this book.
d. that we remember you.
e. to a young college freshman.
f. was serious.
g. this letter.
h. to warn students.
i. make this decision.
j. the area where the item was lost.

B. 1. Tell us about your school activities.
    2. Did you ever lose an item in school?
    3. What did you do to reclaim the lost item?
    4. Tell us about a letter you received.

C. Tell us what you think when I say:

lost and found - director of student activities - possessions - trust - decision - manuscript - crowds

D. Describe what you see in the picture below.

E. Read the poem aloud. Answer orally the questions listed following poem.

Beautiful Soul

Her face, I don't know
where it was that he had
seen it first, or did he
see that which he sought [1]   [1] looked for

What matters most, is
that in her sweet
expression he suddenly
perceived [2] *the goodness of humanity*   [2] saw

And now, he shall no longer
ask if there's some truth
to what they call the
"decent [3] *kind." For now,*   [3] good

no measure of denial [4]   [4] saying "no"
can feign [5] *destroy that*   [5] assume
which his eyes perceived
across the way... serene [6] *and kind...*   [6] peaceful

1. Identify the person speaking in the first verse.
2. Identify the relative pronouns in this poem.
3. Does the title express the main idea of the poem?
4. Who is the "Beautiful Soul" of this poem? Discuss it in class.
5. What idea is expressed in the first verse? Discuss this in class.
6. Does this poem appear sad or happy? Discuss it in class.

Appendix

The Principal Parts of Irregular Verbs

A complete list of **irregular** verbs and their principal parts can be found in every good dictionary. Included here for the convenience of the reader are some more commonly used irregular verbs and their principal parts. The first principal part of a verb is the **infinitive** (simple form of the verb), the second principal part is the **past tense** and the third principal part is the **past participle**. We don't ordinarily consider the **present participle** to be one of the principal parts because it is always regular and is quite simple to construct ; i.e., be = being, go = going, have = having, do = doing, etc.

Infinitive	Past Tense	Past Participle
awake	awaked, awoke	awaked
be	was, were	been
become	became	become
begin	began	begun
bleed	bled	bled
blow	blew	blown
break	broke	broken
bring	brought	brought
build	built	built
buy	bought	bought
catch	caught	caught
choose	chose	chosen
come	came	come
deal	dealt	dealt
dig	dug	dug
dive	dived, dove	dived
do	did	done
draw	drew	drawn
dream	dreamt, dreamed	dreamt, dreamed
drink	drank	drunk
drive	drove	driven
eat	ate	ate
fall	fell	fallen
feel	felt	felt
fight	fought	fought
find	found	found
fly	flew	flown
forget	forgot	forgot, forgotten
forgive	forgave	forgiven
get	got	got, gotten
give	gave	given
go	went	gone
grow	grew	grown
hang	hung, hanged	hung, hanged

have	had	had
hear	heard	heard
hide	hid	hidden
hold	held	held
keep	kept	kept
know	knew	known
lay	laid	laid
leave	left	left
lie (recline)	lay	lain
lie (tell a lie)	lied	lied
lose	lost	lost
make	made	made
meet	met	met
pay	paid	paid
read	read	rcad
run	ran	run
say	said	said
see	saw	seen
sell	sold	sold
send	sent	sent
shoot	shot	shot
sing	sang	sung
sit	sat	sat
sleep	slept	slept
speak	spoke	spoken
speed	sped	sped
spend	spent	spent
stand	stood	stood
steal	stole	stolen
swim	swam	swum
take	took	taken
teach	taught	taught
tell	told	told
think	thought	thought
throw	threw	thrown

understand	understood	understood
wake	waked, woke	woke
wear	wore	worn
win	won	won
wind	wound	wound
withdraw	withdrew	withdrawn
write	wrote	written

II. Parts of Speech

This brief glossary serves the purpose of a rapid review of the parts of speech in their most common usage. Most of the material described here has been discussed in detail within appropriate chapters of the book. Some definitions are followed by typical examples of usage.

A. The NOUN is a word that names a **person, place, thing, quality, state of being** or **action**. The noun has **number, gender** and **case**. It is used in every complete sentence as a subject. There are concrete (physical) nouns and there are abstract (idea) nouns. Examples : concrete = table, book, bread ; abstract = happiness, love, thought.

B. The PRONOUN is a **substitute for a noun** or a noun equivalent. There are several kinds of pronouns :

1. The Personal Pronoun-I, you, he, she, we, etc.

2. The Demonstrative Pronoun-this, that, these, those

3. The Indefinite Pronoun-anybody, somebody, many, each, one, some, etc.

4. The Relative Pronoun-that, who, which, etc.

5. The Interrogative Pronoun-who?, which?, what?, etc.

6. The Reflexive Pronoun-myself, yourself, etc.

C. The VERB usually tells something about the **action** of the subject. The verb may also express **condition** or **state of being**. There are four types of verbs :

    1. The Transitive Verb-tells what the subject does to an object, a person, a thing or a place.

    2. The Intransitive Verb-does not need an object to complete its meaning. The intransitive verb tells something about what the subject is.

    3. The Linking Verb-is a special kind of intransitive verb. It functions as a connection between a **subject** and a **predicate complement**.

    4. The Auxiliary Verb-helps other verbs to express **action** or **condition** or **state** of **being**.

D. The ADJECTIVE describes a noun or a pronoun. It is neither singular nor plural. The adjective can compare one noun to another. Adjectives are classified according to their function :

    1. The Descriptive Adjective-**describes** the noun or the pronoun.

    2. The Limiting Adjective-**limits** or **defines** the meaning of the noun or the pronoun.

E. The ARTICLE comes in two forms :

    1. The Definite Article-the

    2. The Indefinite Article-a, one, an

The is used with a singular or plural noun ; **a** is commonly used with a singular noun.

F. The ADVERB modifies and changes in some way the meaning of a **verb**, an **adjective** or another **adverb**. The following are the most commonly used types of adverbs :

1. The Adverb of TIME-answers the question **when?**, i.e., **recently, soon, immediately, now, then, first, later, always, never, often**, etc.

2. The Adverb of PLACE-answers the question **where?**, i.e., **here, away, west, everywhere**, etc.

3. The Adverb of MANNER-answers the question **how?**, i.e., **quickly, slowly, badly, well**, etc.

G. A PREPOSITION shows the **relationship** between a **noun** or a **pronoun** and another word. The preposition generally expresses the relation of one thing to another in regard to:

1. **time**-i.e. **before** noon, **after** the holidays, **until** midnight, etc.

2. **manner**-i.e. **with** happiness, **by** mistake, etc.

3. **position** or **place**-i.e. **at** the airport, **at** home, **in** the house, **on top of** the mountain, etc.

H. A CONJUNCTION **connects** words or groups of words. There are two types of conjunctions :

1. Coordinating-joins equal grammatical units, i.e. Mary and Kip **and** Susan **and** Joe, Don **or** Sheila, etc. I'll tell you **if and when** I get ready. He'll do it at nine A.M. **or** after ten.

2. Subordinating-introduces a clause that depends on a main or independent clause ; i.e.

    a. **time** (**as, before, when, while**, etc.)

b. **reason** or **cause** (**because, since, why,** etc.)

c. **supposition** or **condition** (**although, unless, whether**.... **or,** etc.)

I. The INTERJECTION serves to express **emotion.** It is generally followed by an **exclamation mark** (!), i.e. OH! HELP! HURRAH! etc.

Active Vocabulary

Words are listed in alphabetical order . The number preceding each word indicates the chapter where it was first used . The synonyms and antonyms are listed in the same manner as they were listed in the pictograph section.

CHAPTER		SYNONYM	ANTONYM
	A		
3	able	adequate	unable
7	above	at a higher place	
4	abuse	maltreatment, hurt	care
3	accept	approve	reject
7	accident	mishap	purpose
7	accompany	escort	be alone
5	accomplish	achieve	give up
5	accountable	responsible	irresponsible
3	accusing	incriminating	
5	achieve	accomplish	fail
9	across	through	
3	activity	action, function	inactivity
9	adjust	adapt	disturb
5	admonish	warn	
3	adopt	support	discard
10	advantage	make the best (of it)	
10	advise	counsel	

2	afraid	frightened	unafraid
4	affectionate	tender	indifferent
8	afford	have the money for	
3	against	opposed	for
3	age	oldness, time	youth
4	agency	department	
5	agree	be satisfied	be dissatisfied
5	ahead	foremost	behind
10	aim	try	
8	alien	immigrant	citizen
3	allow	permit	deny
1	also	too	
9	altogether	completely	
6	amazed	surprised, puzzled	unamazed
6	ancestor	forebear	descendant
9	ancient	very old	
7	ankle	joint between foot and leg	
7	annual	yearly	
6	anticipation	expectation	
4	anxiety	fear	contentment
5	anyway	anyhow	
8	apologize	express regret	blame
2	appear	become visible	disappear
5	applause	acclamation	criticism
4	approach	come closer	
2	area	spot	
10	around	about	
1	arrive	come	depart
10	article	thing, report	
6	ascent	going up	
1	assemble	gather	scatter
9	associate	be friends	disassociate
7	assume	suppose	know

3	assure	promise, guarantee	mislead
1	atmosphere	feeling	
4	attack	assault, use force	aid, defend
3	attend	be present	be absent
3	attentively	closely	negligently
5	attire	dress	undress
2	attorney	lawyer	
3	authority	power	subordination
4	available	accessible	
3	avoid	shun	consent
5	aware	sensible	unaware
8	away	gone	
1	awe	reverence	irreverence

B

9	background	environment	
7	bag	sac	
5	ballot	voting sheet	
6	banish	exile	shelter
6	bathe	wash	
2	be still	at rest	be active
2	before	prior to	after
1	begin	start	end
2	behave	obey	misbehave
9	belief	faith	disbelief
3	belong	have a proper place	
6	below	lower place	lose
3	benefit	profit	
8	besides	anyway	
7	between	in the space that separates two things	
3	beyond	past	near
9	biased	prejudiced	fair
2	bitterness	sadness	joy

9	birth	beginning	
2	blanket	covering	
9	blessing	benediction	curse
7	blinded	cannot see	
8	blush	become red in the face	
2	boat	vessel	
9	border	boundary	interior
7	bottom	the lowest place	
9	bound	united	
10	box	container	
3	break into	make illegal entry	
3	break out	begin	end
7	bridge	span	
2	bring	fetch	send
7	broad	wide	narrow
4	bruise	black and blue spot, injury	
3	busing	transporting	

C

2	cabin	cottage	mansion
1	cafeteria	restaurant	
3	call	phone	
3	call on	visit	
5	campaign	work in the election	
2	camping	outing	
5	candidate	nominee	
2	canoe	boat	
4	capacity	ability, maximum	inability
7	care	be concerned	
7	careless	reckless, negligent	careful
2	carry	transport	
7	cave	underground chamber	

5	caution	warn	disregard
4	cease	stop	continue
8	celebrate	observe festivities joyfully	
8	ceremony	ritual	
8	chairman	director	
5	chance	opportunity	plan
5	change	alter, become different	retain, remain the same
9	charitable	benevolent	selfish
10	check	examine	
5	choice	many to pick from	limited selection
2	chore	task, job	
3	circumstance	occurrence, condition	planned action
8	citizenship	become citizen	
10	claim	identify as one's own	disclaim
1	class	group of students	
1	classroom	schoolroom	
3	clean	sanitary	dirty
6	clear	transparent	muddy
7	clearly	plainly	indistinctly
6	climb	ascend	descend
5	close	near	far
4	clumsy	awkward	graceful
10	collect	gather	distribute
6	colorless	lacking hue	colorful
1	come	arrive	go
5	common	everyone's, related	uncommon
6	community	society	disunity
4	complain	whine	approve
5	complete	total	incomplete
6	completely	entirely	not at all
2	concern	worry	unconcern
5	concerned	nervous	indifferent
10	concerning	in regard (to)	

5	condemn	judge	
6	conclude	decide, finish	
3	confused	perplexed	orderly
5	conscious of	realistic	unrealistic
5	constant	always	seldom
3	constitutional	inherent	
5	continue	persist, go on	cease
6	contrary	opposite	
3	contribute	donate	receive
2	control	balance	
3	convicted	found guilty	acquitted
5	convince	persuade	dissuade
5	cooperate	work together	oppose
5	council	planning body	
3	counsel	advise	deter
2	countryside	rural area	municipality
3	court	tribunal	
4	cruelty	brutality	
7	crawl	creep	run
6	creature	being	
2	cross	angry	happy
7	crowbar	a long iron bar	
10	crowd	number of people	
4	cruel	inhuman	gentle
4	cry	weep	laugh
7	crystalline	clear	unclear
6	curious	inquiring	indifferent
1	custom	fashion	

D

6	danger	peril	safety
7	dark	obscure	light
7	debris	rubble	
10	decent	good	evil, bad
6	decide	determine	doubt

10	decision	determination	indecision
3	declare	advise	stifle
7	deep	profound	shallow
3	deep	profound	Shallow
6	defy	go against	
1	delay	detain, postpone	hasten
3	deliberate	consider	
5	deliver	give	take
7	demand	order	
9	democracy	government by the people	
10	denial	refusal	
8	department	section	
7	deputy	representative of law enforcement	
8	descent	origin	
2	desperately	hopelessly	hopefully
6	despise	hate	
4	destined	fated	
4	develop	grow	deteriorate
9	difference	dissimilarity	similarity
1	different	unlike, diverse	same
4	difficult	hard	east
7	dig	excavate	bury
10	direction	toward	
4	dirty	filthy	clean
2	discomfort	annoyance	contentment
7	discover	find	search
10	discussion	talk	
2	distance	remoteness, land space	closeness
4	distrust	suspicion, doubt	trust
4	disturb	interfere (with)	
2	dive	plunge	
3	doubt	uncertainty	certainty

7	downward	to a lower place	upward
7	draft	current	
2	drag	pull	
5	dress	clothe	undress
2	drip	drop	
8	drop in	visit	depart
2	drown	sink	stay afloat
1	during	while	
5	duty	responsibility	freedom

E

1	eager	anxious	indifferent
1	early	near beginning	late
7	echo	reverberation	
9	element	principle	
6	else	differently, more	
8	embarrass	perplex	relieve
8	embrace	hug	recoil
7	emerge	come out	go in
4	emotional	agitated	calm
6	enchanted	charmed	disenchanted
5	encourage	support	discourage
9	endeavor	work	idleness
10	enjoy	get pleasure (from)	
5	entire	whole	partial
6	envious	jealous	satisfied
3	equal	same	unequal
4	especially	particularly	
8	establish	secure	break up
9	ethnic	cultural	
4	evident	clear, easy to see	concealed
7	examine	investigate	answer
7	except	excluded	
4	excited	enthusiastic	passive
2	exclaim	cry out	be silent

6	exist	live	die
8	expensive	costly	
7	experience	try, do	
6	explain	tell clearly	obscure
7	explore	investigate	ignore
4	extraordinary	remarkable	common

F

4	face it	cope	avoid
10	factor	element	
7	fall	drop down	
8	fall on	come out on	
2	falls	waterfalls	
7	far	distant	
1	fathom	understand	
4	fear	dread	trust
4	feel	be concerned	ignore
10	feel free	don't hesitate	
4	feeling	sensation	
9	fellow man	person	
9	fertile	fruitful	arid
5	fine	good	bad
5	finish	end	start
3	first	original	last
2	foam	froth	
6	foggy	misty	clear
3	follow	succeed	precede
8	following	next	previous
7	footing	support	
5	forceful	powerful	weak
7	formation	rock origin	
9	fortune	wealth	poverty
6	forward	ahead	backward
10	forward	send	keep
4	foster	adopted	

4	found	discovered, recovered	lost
7	fracture	break	mend
9	freedom	liberty	
1	freeway	expressway	
10	freshman	beginning student	
1	friend		enemy
1	friendly	amicable	unfriendly
10	full	filled	empty
1	funny	strange	serious
7	further	more distant	

G

8	gathering	meeting	
3	gavel	a wooden hammer	
1	get acquainted	meet	avoid
5	get ahead	progress	fall behind
7	give up	quit	
1	glad	happy, pleased	sad
9	goal	intention	
10	gone	lost	
5	good behavior	good conduct	misbehavior
3	goods	property, merchandise	
6	gossip	spread rumor	be discrete
4	gradual	step by step	sudden
6	greedy	avaricious	generous
7	grizzly	grey bear	
2	groceries	food	
2	ground	place, surface	
3	guard	sentry	
4	guess	suppose	be certain
3	guilty	at fault	innocent

H

5	habit	custom	
4	had better	ought to	
4	hallway	corridor	
7	halt	end	continue
5	hard	difficult to bear	easy-going
7	hasten	hurry	slow down
6	hate	detest	love
1	have	possess	lack
4	health	well-being	sickness
2	hear	listen	be deaf
8	heartily	sincerely	insincerely
2	help	assist	hinder
9	heritage	tradition	
2	hesitation	pause	haste
2	hilly	uneven terrain	flat land
7	hit	strike	
2	hold on	grip	
7	hole	opening	
9	homeland	country of residence	
2	hope	a feeling of anticipation	
4	hospitality	cordiality	
3	household	family	
3	housekeeping	management of a house	
2	housewife	married woman in charge of a household	career woman
6	huge	enormous	diminutive
4	hysterical	uncontrolled	calm

I

10	identifying	recognition	
5	idol	image	
4	illness	sickness	health
6	imitation	copy	
7	immediately	at once	later
6	immense	enormous	tiny
9	immigrant	settler	emigrant
10	impatient	restless	patient
5	important	significant	insignificant
5	impress	affect	undo
8	impressive	imposing	unimpressive
8	improve	better	worsen
5	in front of	before	behind
9	in search (of)	trying to find	
10	in touch	close	
8	in vain	without value	
9	inalienable	indisputable	disputable
3	income	salary, earning	expenses
6	incorrigible	hopeless	hopeful
4	increase	grow	diminish
7	indicated	specified	unspecified
4	ineffable	inexpressible	
2	inexpensive	simple	ostentatious
4	infant	child	adult
6	inhabitant	occupant	
7	injury	damage	
3	innocence	lack of guilt	guilt
6	inquiry	question	statement
5	insist	maintain	yield
6	instead	in place of	
3	intend	have in mind	
1	interesting	fascinating	boring
4	interfere	come between	not become involved
3	investigation	examination	

6	involved	confused, intricate	simple
10	item	article	

J

1	jam	overcrowding	
8	job	work	
8	join	get together (with)	
7	joke	josh	be serious
4	joy	happiness	unhappiness
8	judgment	decision	
2	junior high	middle school	

K

10	kept	held	
3	kind	sympathetic	unkind
1	know	understand	unhappiness
8	knowledge	understanding	
4	known	public	

L

7	labyrinth	maze	straight passage
4	lack	want	supply
7	ladder	cord steps	
6	lake	large body of water	
7	lamp	a device for making light	
8	large	big	
2	late	delayed	early
5	lately	recently	long ago
1	laugh	chuckle	cry
2	law	rule	disorder
9	leadership	guidance	
4	learn	be informed by	ignore
3	least	minimum	most
4	leave	depart	return

6	left	alone, by herself	
1	lesson	instruction	
5	let	allow	refuse
4	life-span	lifetime	
1	like	fond of	dislike
5	likewise	also	otherwise
1	listen	hear	ignore
2	living quarters	residence	
7	location	place	displacement
4	lock	confine	open
8	look for	search	
6	look forward to	to anticipate	dread
2	lose	fail to keep	gain
10	lost	left behind	found
6	lost her way	got confused	
6	loud	noisy	quiet
4	love	affection	hatred
3	low	small, little	high
7	lower	let down, reduce	raise
7	lucky	fortunate	unfortunate

M

5	maintain	keep, defend	drop
2	make up	compensate	lack
4	manners	habitual or customary behavior	
10	manuscript	book	
1	many	a lot	few
1	map	chart	
10	mark	sign	
9	marry	wed	divorce
2	marshmallows	soft candy	
4	mature	grown up	immature
4	maybe	perhaps	impossible
2	meditation	contemplation	

8	meeting	getting together	
4	memory	recollection	
3	mercy	pity	severity
5	merry-go-round	coming and going	
2	mile	1.6 kilometers	
8	minor	secondary	major
2	minute	moment	
8	miss	regret the absence (of)	
4	mistreat	injure	care for
1	morning	early in the day	evening
4	mortality	death	immortality
3	most	greatest	least
6	mountain	large hill	valley
6	move	stir	rest
7	multiply	increase	decrease
4	mysterious	secret	obvious

N

1	name	title	
7	narrow	tight	wide
2	near	close	distant
5	neat	elegant, nice	clumsy
4	neck	the part of man joining the head and body	
1	need	want	option
4	needed	desired	
4	neglect	disregard	care
9	newcomer	recent arrival	
6	no end	very much	
5	noise	clamor	stillness
3	note	remark	
5	notice	pay attention	neglect

O

3	oath	solemn promise	
8	occasion	opportunity	
2	occupation	line of work	leisure
3	offer	give	rescind
2	officer	official	
1	often	frequently	seldom
3	old	aged	young
4	open	show her feelings	withdrawn
9	opinion	view	
5	opponent	adversary	friend
9	opportunity	good chance	
3	order	command	
6	originality	creativity	
3	orphanage	institution for children without parents	
4	overcome	conquer	succumb to
3	overcrowded	congested	spacious
8	overheard	heard secretly	
2	overturn	tip over	
2	own	possess, themselves	lack

P

4	pack	put things together	unpack
2	paddle	move the canoe	
2	pain	hurt	
1	part	section	whole
10	pass it on	tell it	
7	passage	narrow way, corridor	
9	passport	document for travel	
3	peer	equal	unequal
10	perceive	see	
6	perfect	faultless	imperfect
3	personal	private	public
3	philanthropist	humanitarian	misanthrope

4	physical	bodily	emotional
2	picnic	outing	
1	place	locality	nowhere
3	place in custody	legal guardianship	
7	plan	arrange	chance
3	plea	request	
5	pledge	promise	refuse
3	point at	single out, show	
5	popular	favorite	unpopular
8	position	post	
10	possession	belonging	
7	precaution	care	carelessness
6	prejudice	bigotry	fairness
7	preparation	arrangement	unpreparedness
2	prepare	fix, make ready	
6	presence	being there	
9	present	show	
4	previous	prior	subsequent
4	problem	difficulty	solution
10	promise	pledge, assure	
1	pronounce	articulate	
8	proper	appropriate	improper
3	prosecuting	public official	
9	proud	self-satisfied, joyful	ashamed
5	proudly	with pride	humbly
10	publication date	date the finished book is offered to the public	
7	pull	tow	push
6	pulsate	vibrate	
4	pulse	heartbeat	
6	punish	chastise	reward
9	pursuit	striving	avoiding
6	push	shove, force	
5	puzzled	confused	clear

Q

5	qualification	capability	inability
4	quick	fast	slow
4	quicken	accelerate	slow down
3	quickly	rapidly	slowly
3	quietly	silently, softly	noisily

R

3	rap	tap	
2	rapids	rushing water	
6	reach	arrive at	revert
3	reasonable	rational	unreasonable
9	recently	lately, not long ago	long ago
3	recess	pause	
3	reconvene	meet again	recess
6	refuse	garbage	
4	refuse	decline	accept
1	relative	kinsman	stranger
1	relaxed	rested tense	tense
7	release	free	confine
9	religion	belief	
7	relieve	secure	
4	reluctant	hesitant	willing
4	remain	continue	discontinue
5	remark	notice	disregard
7	remind	make (someone) remember	
2	rent	pay for the use of	
6	repeater	someone who does something again	
4	reply	answer	ignore
4	request	proposal, petition	
8	required	necessary	unnecessary
10	resale	sell back	buy back
7	rescue	save	endanger

8	residence	habitation, living in one place	
9	respect	regard	abuse
2	respond	answer	ignore
5	response	reply, answer	
5	responsibility	duty	
2	rest	relax	work
4	return	come back	leave
3	reveal	disclose	cover up
6	rhythmically	in a pattern	
9	riches	wealth	poverty
2	ride	transport, float on water	
10	ridiculous	not sensible	
3	right	prerogative	
8	risk	chance	
2	river	stream of water	
7	rock	large stone	
7	rope	cord	
4	rough	boisterous	gentle
2	run	flow	
4	run away	go away, escape	stay
5	run for	be in a race	

S

9	sacrifice	loss	profit
4	sad	depressed	happy
2	safe	out of danger, secure	unsafe
1	sage	wise man	
9	sail	travel by boat	
2	sandwich	slice of bread with a filling of meat or cheese, etc .	
8	save	redeem	lose

5	scorn	ridicule	respect
7	search	look for	discover
4	see	appear	conceal
3	seek	look for	find
3	seem	appear, look like	
5	select	pick	ignore, overlook
8	sell	trade for money	buy
5	sense	feel	ignore
3	sentence	judgment	acquittal
10	serene	peaceful	restless
6	serious	earnest	funny
9	setback	obstacle	advancement
9	settle	establish oneself	move on
6	severely	harshly	leniently
7	shade	shadow	
6	shapeless	formless	formed
7	sheriff	county law enforcement officer	
8	shop	select	sell
2	short	small	long
1	show	point out	hide
7	show up	return, come back	
6	side	edge	center
6	sight	seeing	blindness
8	sign	contract	
4	silent	quiet	loud
9	similar	same	different
6	simple	uncomplicated	complicated
4	sincere	honest	feigned
7	skeleton	bony framework	
5	slow down	ease up	speed up
2	smile	grin	frown
4	social	public	personal
9	social class	rank of people	
4	sofa	couch	

3	somebody	someone	nobody
3	something	anything	nothing
4	soul	spirit	
5	sound	seem	
9	span	extend	
8	spare	omit	
4	speechless	without words	talkative
7	spelunking	cave exploring	
5	splendid	magnificent	
8	sponsor	support, be responsible	
6	spot	place	
7	sprained	twisted	
6	spread	circulate	
5	stage	platform	
8	stammer	stutter	
6	stand	tolerate	
1	stand up	get up	sit down
5	state	say	
8	stay out	live somewhere else	
3	steal	take without permission	
6	step up	walk over	
3	stern	severe	lenient
2	stolen	lifted	bought
2	stop	halt	go
5	strive	labor	loaf
2	strong	powerful	
5	stubborn	obstinate	docile
1	student	pupil	teacher
1	study	learn	
8	subject	task	
8	success	good result	
2	suddenly	abruptly, unexpectedly	slowly

9	suffer	endure, tolerate	enjoy
5	suggest	hint	declare
10	suggestion	hint, idea	
2	supermarket	grocery store	
2	supper	evening meal	breakfast
5	sure	certain	uncertain
7	surface	exterior	
6	surprise	astonish	forewarn
6	surround	encircle	
3	suspend	dismiss	
3	sustain	support	release
5	sway	affect	
8	swearing in	oath taking	
2	swim	stay afloat	sink
5	system	order	disorder

T

3	tackle	player in football	
3	take over	assume control	lose
1	tale	story	
6	tall	high	short
1	teacher	instructor	student
3	team	group	individual
4	tension	anxiety	relaxation
4	terminal	incurable	curable
7	terrific	intense	
3	testify	witness, give evidence	
1	think	reason	
3	thorough	complete	careless
6	throng	crowd	
7	throughout	everywhere	
7	tie	secure	untie
2	tip over	overturn	stay upright
2	toast	fry	

3	together	jointly	separately
9	tolerant	understanding	intolerant
6	top	summit	bottom
2	toss	fling	catch
9	tough	able to take adversity	soft
2	toward	in the direction of	away from
3	town	small city	metropolis
1	traffic	cars, trucks, etc .	
1	traffic jam	transportation stoppage	
5	transition	change	
9	transport	carry	
1	travel	journey	stay home
4	treat	handle	
2	tremble	shake	be still
7	trip	journey	
3	trouble	difficulty	tranquility
8	trust	have faith, believe	mistrust
6	try	attempt	abandon
2	turn back	turn around	go ahead
4	twinkle	sparkle	be expressionless
7	twisting	curving	straight
2	typical	normal	unusual

U

1	unable	incompetent	able
8	unaccustomed	not used to	accustomed
2	under	beneath	on top
9	underneath	beneath	above
4	understanding	sympathy	cruelty
8	unfriendly	unkind	
9	unlike	different	same
6	unknown	unfamiliar	known
4	until	before, up to now	afterward
9	untrustworthy	unreliable	trustworthy

5	upcoming	next, future	
7	upward	to a higher place	
10	urgent	important	unimportant
9	used to	accustomed (to)	unaccustomed (to)
4	useful	helpful	useless

V

1	vacation	holiday, rest	work
6	vaguely	indefinitely	definitely
10	value	worth	uselessness
3	varsity	the main team	
7	vast	immense, great	small
3	victim	prey	aggressor
1	visit	go to see (someone)	
4	visitor	guest	
5	voice	choice	
5	vote	decide	

W

7	waist	body above hips	
1	wait	linger, stay (in place)	leave
4	wander	stroll about aimlessly	walk purposefully
3	war	conflict	peace
4	ward	adopted person	
3	warehouse	storage building	
2	warm	hot	cold
10	warn	caution	
9	wealth	riches	poverty
7	wedge	constrict	release
2	weekend	Saturday and Sunday	weekday
6	welcome	acceptable	unwelcome
4	welfare	social service	
9	well-established	respected	
3	well-to-do	rich	poor
2	wet	moist	dry

1	whisper	soft voice sound	
5	wide	broad	narrow
1	wisdom	knowledge	
4	withdraw	retreat	emerge
5	win	get	lose
6	work	labor	rest
1	world	earth	
2	worry	concern	unconcern
3	worse	more unfavorable	better
9	worship	pray	blaspheme
10	worth	value	
3	wrong	error	right
3	wrong side of the tracks	ill-bred	well-bred

Y

2	yell	shout	whisper
2	young	youthful	old

Index